Stay
Confident

other titles in the Kogan Page creating success series

THE SUNDAY TIMES

Stay
Confident

John Caunt

ATING SUCCESS

First published in 2001
Reprinted in 2002, 2004

Kogan Page Limited
120 Pentonville Road
London N1 9JN

British Library Cataloguing in Publication Data

A CIP record for this book is available from the British Library.

ISBN 0 7494 3526 7

Typeset by Jean Cussons Typesetting, Diss, Norfolk
Printed and bound in Great Britain by Clays Ltd, St Ives plc

contents

introduction

All you need in life is ignorance and confidence and success is sure.

Mark Twain

Skill and confidence are an unconquered army.

George Herbert

No prizes for spotting the common denominator. Confidence is fundamental to successful performance – as important, in my belief, as skill and knowledge. Even though I would not go as far as Mark Twain, I have seen more skilled people fall by the wayside as a result of diminished confidence than confident people go under through lack of skill.

why is confidence so important to success?

Confident people enjoy change. They trust themselves to be able to weather it and believe in their capacity to succeed. They are able to take risks and to see difficult tasks as challenges rather than threats. They are prepared to persevere when things are not going right and the experience of failure does not floor them. On the other hand, people who doubt their capabilities steer clear of tough tasks and challenges. They give up in the face of setbacks and set their sights low. Rather than believing in success they concentrate on what will happen when they fail. As a consequence they remain firmly within the comfort zone, secure but not achieving very much.

For many of us, it is not so much initial self-belief that is the problem as hanging on to our confidence in the face of all the difficulties we experience. What we find hard is the resilience factor – the ability to bounce back after slights, setbacks and stressful events. We start our careers full of enthusiasm and sure of our abilities to handle what is thrown at us but, over time, we are worn down by the battering we get from events, pressures and changes. In the modern workplace those pressures come thick and fast as we battle to cope with escalating workloads, greater regulation, new practices, increased responsibility and ever more uncertainty. They have the effect of exacerbating interpersonal difficulties, heightening our fears and lowering our sense of being in control. So the main thrust of this book is about preserving confidence – how to strengthen your resilience and overcome the challenges you are likely to meet in your working life.

Stay Confident is not aimed at people occupying a particular level of responsibility. We can suffer from confidence dips at any stage in our careers. Some readers will have management or supervisory responsibilities, whereas others may be independent professionals or holders of more junior posts. While the book's focus is very clearly upon the workplace, I would not wish to present the impression that confidence comes in neat separate parcels, each exclusive to a certain aspect of our lives. Successes or setbacks in one area may have a significant impact upon others. At some points in the book I make specific reference to such topics as the balance of work, leisure and family life. Elsewhere, please take as read the intention that strategies discussed in relation to work may have more general applicability.

Of course, confidence does not flow in a constant and convenient way like electricity or water supplies. It comes and goes in irritating fits and starts. You may be comfortable and sure of yourself in one situation, but self-conscious and insecure in another. Tasks that might normally be a breeze for you can become intimidating when you are stressed and overloaded. You can never be completely sure when your confidence is going to be threatened, and that makes it all the more important that you are adequately prepared to weather the challenges and come out of them smiling.

what are the things that threaten our confidence at work?

The first assault on our self-belief comes from people – the bullies, critics and straightforward cussed creatures who knowingly or unwittingly blight our daily lives. In the course of several chapters we will look at how to handle challenging interpersonal situations as well as building supportive relationships that can see us through difficult times.

Next comes the self-inflicted damage. We chastise ourselves for our mistakes and failings, load ourselves with unrealistic expectations and exaggerate our fears and worries. We will consider how to counteract such self-generated negative activity, and will see how effective presentation and calm, assertive behaviour can not only persuade others of our self-assurance, but can convince ourselves too.

Third there are events. We will look at strategies for dealing with setbacks and crises, and reducing the stress that is so much a part of contemporary working life.

And finally, there is lack of planning and direction. We will see that clarity about where we are heading and focus on where to direct our energies can greatly increase our sense of being in control.

This sense of control is a major ingredient of self-belief and forms a recurrent theme throughout the book. Being in control is about the extent to which we feel in charge of our working lives – how far we are able to influence what happens to us. Do we have authority over our actions and reactions or are we being helplessly swept along? It's about what we attach importance to and how we react to people and situations. It doesn't mean seeking to direct others, but rather making sure that we don't hand control of our confidence to them. Too often we do this by allowing ourselves to be unduly affected by other people's behaviour and attitudes.

Perhaps most importantly, being in control is to do with how we think about ourselves. It's a matter of being realistic – owning up to our weaknesses and doing something about them – but also of taking full account of the evidence that contradicts our irrational fears, worries and negative self-talk. It means working to promote our positive attitudes and trusting ourselves to succeed.

where are you heading?

Confident people tend to have a clear sense of where they are going. They know what is important to them and what they are trying to achieve. They are clear about the skills they may need to develop in order to get there and the obstacles they will need to overcome. And they are supported in the pursuit of their goals by a healthy appraisal of previous achievements. Even if we have previously examined all these things, it is easy in the hurly-burly of our working lives to lose sight of them or to remain locked into a set of assumptions that no longer represent our most important aspirations. This chapter is therefore about re-establishing that sense of direction that we all need if we are to succeed.

needs and preferences

What is important to you in your job? Some people are prepared to tolerate very disagreeable conditions provided they are sufficiently well rewarded. For others, creative challenge, social factors, respect within the community or the ability to influence others are more important. Awareness of what motivates you is a valuable confidence-building block. It can help you to make the right decisions at important junctures in your working life, and can assist you in steering your activities towards those things that are going to give you the greatest measure of satisfaction. However, it's possible to become so bound up in just doing the job that you neglect the need to step back occasionally and examine what it is that moves you. The following exercise offers a simple way of addressing this.

Select from the list below the 10 items that are most important to you in a work setting. Don't just think of those things that are important in the job you are doing at the moment, but the features that you would ideally seek in any job.

honesty	commitment
learning	excellence
creativity	acceptance
status	freedom
friendship	money
loyalty	influence
achievement	appreciation
teamwork	challenge
security	excitement
harmony	comfort
respect	risk
integrity	competition
fun	predictability
health	vitality
curiosity	contribution
structure	responsibility

The list is just a prompt to your thoughts; there is nothing magic about the words I have chosen. If you think of other words that seem more appropriate to you, include them in your choice of 10. But do give the exercise some thought, and be honest with yourself.

Now arrange the 10 items in order of their importance to you (1 = most important, 10 = least important). Few of us fit neatly into categories, so there is no scoring or bracketing system for this exercise, but the resulting list should give you a fair idea of your most powerful needs and preferences. If, for example, words like friendship, harmony, fun and teamwork feature strongly, it may suggest a need for affiliation that could make you uncomfortable with situations where you have to work in isolation or in managerial circumstances where you may need to make unpopular decisions. If honesty and integrity are high up on your list, you will be unhappy in any role that requires you to be economical with the truth. Examine your list and consider what it says about you.

---

ask yourself:

■ Is there any mismatch between the preferences I have identified and the day-to-day realities of my working life?

■ If so, how might I seek to change my work or the way I do it to achieve greater harmony between preferences and workplace realities?

---

achievements

Achievements represent solid ground on which you can build confidence. They provide you with a foothold on those occasions when self-doubt starts to creep over you, and provided you don't use them as excuses for complacency will act as stepping-stones to still greater levels of attainment. So it's well worth spending some time reflecting upon them. Producing an achievement list is a good way to do this. Putting your achievements down on paper is a lot more meaningful than just thinking about them. It gives you a reference you can return to and update. If you are customarily self-deprecating or not brimful of confidence, you are unlikely at first to find this the most comfortable task in the world. The list seems so thin to start with. Many people struggle to find more than a handful of things they consider achievements, and regard even the ones they identify as pretty pathetic. Part of this is down to natural reluctance to blow your own trumpet, but it's also about the way we characterise achievements. We tend to think only of those that have been marked by some form of public recognition – qualification milestones, job promotions, awards. But the achievements that should matter most in confidence terms are those that may be known only to ourselves.

It is an achievement:

- ▓ every time you face up to fear;
- ▓ every time you confront a problem;
- ▓ every time you handle a difficult situation;
- ▓ every time you bounce back from a disappointment.

We often misperceive such occasions as failures because they are associated with some discomfort, and we tend to remember just the bad things about the situation – the anxiety, fear or disappointment. So dig out those real achievements, large and small. And don't feel self-conscious about writing them down; there's nobody looking over your shoulder. As you become more accustomed to recording your accomplishments it becomes easier and more natural.

Don't just think about achievements at work. Provided you are prepared to make a conscious connection, there is a confidence spillover between achievements in different aspects of our lives. So, whatever the achievements – facing up to your fear of heights on a climbing wall, handling a tricky family problem – put them down. If they are meaningful to you, they can act as references.

Using the following headings may help to jog your memory about achievements in different areas of your life:

■ home and family;
■ education;
■ work;
■ leisure and personal development;
■ contribution and community.

goals

You may already have a number of stated goals in relation to your job, but how far were they determined by you, and do they reflect the full range of your aspirations? It may be that all you currently have are narrow performance targets and objectives. Nothing whatsoever wrong with these, but they don't encompass the full range of outcomes and experiences that give your job meaning and satisfaction. There is value in setting personal and career development goals that correspond with those things you have already identified as being important in your work.

Before going any further, ask yourself what those goals might be. Just jot down what you would like to achieve over the next couple of years. No need to go into detail at this stage. We will spend the rest of the chapter looking at how you may refine these draft goals, and set about making them achievable.

Personal goals can play a significant part in helping to develop and maintain confidence. They are *your* goals – control is in *your* hands. They give a structure and purpose that is individual to you. However, they are tools that must be up to the job. If they are to be so, there are five requirements you should bear in mind: clarity, realism, economy, activity and means. If you want a mnemonic for this, then it has to be CREAM:

■ **Clarity**
You need to be clear about:
   – what it is you are aiming to achieve;

–   by when you hope to achieve it;
–   how you will know that you have got there.

You don't have to go overboard trying to achieve total precision, but do make sure that goals are specific enough for you to be able to identify the activities necessary to bring about their achievement, and that they have a clear end point and associated deadline.

▓ **Realism**

Setting goals that are too demanding is a common mistake. Having a vision of where you want to get eventually is fine, but your immediate goals should be just out of your reach. It's a matter of having to stretch to achieve them but not to saddle yourself with aspirations that will be impossible to achieve in the time-scale. Remember that failure to meet your goals may result in damage to confidence. Of course, it's an equal mistake to make your goals too easy. If there is minimal effort involved in achieving them, they will be meaningless.

▓ **Economy**

Don't set yourself too many goals within a given time period. You won't be able to give them all the necessary attention, and the effect could be the same as setting over-ambitious goals.

▓ **Activity**

Express your goals in positive and active terms. Try to frame them as things you will do rather than things that will happen to you. So, rather than resolving to be promoted in the next 12 months, frame your goal along the lines of: 'to demonstrate that I have the skills to work at a higher level'. It is a matter, once again, of putting yourself in control. Whether or not you are promoted could be dependent on a whole range of factors: somebody else leaving; a restructuring plan that might open up or close down opportunities; an interviewer's preference for another candidate. You cannot control any of these, so stick as far as possible with the things that are in your hands.

▓ **Means**

When you are setting goals, you need to be mindful of the means by which you aim to achieve them. This may require that you learn new skills or achieve a change in behaviour. In some cases the goals them-selves may be new skills and attributes – means to achieve other ends. You also need to be able to break your goals down into smaller units so that you can get a grip on progress towards achieving them.

Let's look at this in a little more detail.

developing skills

As a prompt to your thinking, I have set out below a list of some of the skills that might be important in the achievement of workplace goals or, indeed, might constitute means goals in themselves. Select from the list those it might be necessary for you to work upon, and add any others not on the list that come to mind while you are engaged in the exercise.

assertiveness*	communication skills
decision making	delegating*
developing rapport*	generating enthusiasm
giving feedback*	influencing*
information handling*	listening*
managing disagreements*	meetings management
motivational skills	negotiation
presentation skills	problem solving
project management	questioning and interviewing
setting priorities*	strategic thinking
taking risks	team building
time management*	updating technical competences

Note that those marked with an asterisk are touched upon to some degree in this book, but you will need to give thought at some stage to how others you have identified will be developed. Will it require a guided learning programme or some further reading, or will you be able to achieve the desired results by reflection and practice?

personal qualities

In addition to new skills, the goals you seek may require that you strengthen certain personal qualities, for example: patience; determination; perseverance; flexibility; courage; compassion; objectivity. Take a moment now to identify the qualities you may need to work upon if you are to achieve your goals.

The prospect of changing long-standing traits may appear difficult, but it is quite possible provided you set about it in the right way. Let's assume you have decided that one of the qualities you need to work upon is determination. A general resolution to be more determined is too nebulous to have a great chance of success. So narrow it down. Identify a limited number of instances in which your resolve is most likely to flag – situations involving conflict, for example. Now make a decision that for the next week you will show more determination in such situations. Reward yourself for successfully achieving that limited change of behaviour and extend the period for a month. Once more, reward yourself for sticking to it. Then look for other situations in which increased determination is desirable and work on them in the same way, using your success so far to motivate yourself and reinforce belief in your ability to make the change. Taking the behaviour change in graded steps like this gives you something to get your teeth into and makes it achievable.

overcoming obstacles

As you move towards achievement of your goals you will in all probability have to deal with obstacles in your way. They may come from other individuals and take the form of bullying, criticism or interference. Alternatively, they may be features of the job you do or the organisation you work in, for instance overload, stress or disorganisation. Those common obstacles that have a particular impact on confidence are dealt with in later chapters. You cannot predict with certainty every hindrance you may face, but it is useful at goal-setting stage to be aware of the obvious ones, so that you can be ready with strategies to overcome them.

activity

Having looked at some of the things that need to be borne in mind when setting goals, go back to the rough list you jotted down earlier. Ask yourself:

- Am I still happy that these goals represent the highest priority for me at this time? □
- Do my goals sit comfortably with the preferences I identified at the beginning of this chapter? □
- Is it clear what I want to achieve and by when? □
- Have I framed my goals in such a way that I will know when I have got there? □
- Are my goals adequately stretching but not unrealistic? □
- Have I identified the skills and qualities I will need to work upon and the obstacles I may have to overcome? □
- Are they all achievable in the timescale? □

sub-goals and milestones

OK, you have, let's say, half a dozen goals that you wish to achieve over the next two years. What do you do now? Leaving them as they are and returning every now and again to review progress is seldom sufficient. A goal two years off is just too large, distant and amorphous to permit week-by-week progress. So break it down into manageable stages, each representing a step closer to the end result. Use the end of each stage as a milestone against which you can assess your progress and reward yourself for it. You might like to view the main goal as the pinnacle of a mountain. While you will be keeping your final objective permanently in view, you will also want some way of monitoring your progress and feeling that you are getting somewhere. Sticking with the mountain-climbing analogy, you may also need to explore different routes to the summit, and be prepared to move sideways or even downwards from time to time in order to get around obstacles.

bouncing back

There are always going to be setbacks large and small in your working life:

- You encounter an unexpected problem in an assignment.
- A proposal for additional funding is turned down.
- You are passed over for a promotion.
- You lose an important contract.
- Your job is declared redundant.

We equate setbacks with failure, and the experience of failure causes us to give free rein to negative thoughts. We quail at taking on similar challenges in the future for fear of repeating the experience; we imagine that others are observing our ineptitude, judging and condemning us. And it's a sad fact that failure tends to weigh more heavily with us than success. One perceived flop may give rise to self-doubts that wipe out any number of successes.

But what constitutes failure? Viewed positively, the first two examples above might be seen not as failures, but simply setbacks on the road to achievement – no more than challenges to be overcome. And if these examples can be seen in that way, why not the others too? Certainly, failure to achieve a promotion carries a greater degree of personal disappointment and rejection, and a redundancy compounds these with possible major life changes, but with the right sort of attitude all these can be viewed as challenges rather than reasons to throw in the towel. The fact is that the harshest judges of our performance tend to be ourselves, and the verdicts we reach, which have such an impact on our self-belief, are often based on the flimsiest of evidence. Consider the case study below.

Two months into a new job, Sarah was required to make an important presentation in front of senior managers. She had only made one or two fairly low-key presentations in her previous job and was understandably nervous. She prepared and rehearsed the presentation thoroughly and made sure that visual aids and equipment were up to scratch. Her delivery, although somewhat tense, was quite competent. The senior managers listened to her without comment or question and at the end of the presentation the chairman briefly thanked her. As the group had other business to conduct, she was then required to leave.

By any objective standards Sarah handled the task in a wholly competent and professional manner, but she came away from the experience convinced that she had made a complete mess of it and demonstrated her incompetence to a roomful of senior people. The prospect of ever having to do anything similar filled her with dread, and her sense of failure in this task had an impact on her general confidence.

How could Sarah's judgement be so at variance with reality? The first problem was that Sarah pinned too much of her self-assessment on the reaction of her audience. For her, the presentation was a really big deal, but for her audience it was just one item in a long and tedious meeting. She interpreted their expressionless faces and absence of questions as failure on her part, when in fact they were more the result of an overcrowded agenda and poor meeting management. The curt thanks and requirement that she leave in order to allow the meeting to continue compounded her sense of inadequacy.

Ironically, if members of the group had perceived that Sarah was struggling they might have been more inclined to offer positive feedback, but all they saw was a competent junior manager giving a routine presentation. So clear and thorough was her delivery that there was no need for questions.

Sarah's second misinterpretation arose from the excessively high standards she demanded of herself. Anything less than perfection constituted failure in her eyes, and the small flaws that others may have noted she exaggerated beyond all proportion.

Misinterpretations like this occur day in, day out. We find failure where it hasn't occurred, feel the pain of humiliation and shrink from repeating similar experiences.

Of course, not all our setbacks are the result of misperceptions. We will all face numerous reverses that are unequivocal. But however clear the setback, the sense of failure is still largely of our own making. Even when we have suffered a genuine setback, we are unable to view it as a challenge to start afresh or to change our behaviour, but take it to be something wrong with ourselves. The urge not to repeat the experience is an attempt to reduce the future incidence of failure, but taken to its extreme such a strategy would result in us never taking any risks and never trying anything new – a state of affairs clearly not conducive to any form of achievement, and totally destructive of self-confidence. On the other hand, it makes no sense pointlessly to set yourself up for failure. So we need a strategy that both reduces the incidence of unnecessary setbacks and provides us with the resources to deal with them positively when they do occur. Here are 10 ways to achieve it.

10 ways to minimise and recover from setbacks

1. *Strike a balance between aspiration and realism.* As discussed in Chapter 1, goals need to be stretching but achievable. If you set your goals impossibly high or expect to reach them in one leap, then you set yourself up for failure. However, it is perfectly acceptable to have a target that is well out of reach provided you put in place sub-goals – graduated steps that will enable you to experience a sense of progress as you make your way towards it. As with your goals, don't set performance standards that are too perfectionist. Without settling for substandard, don't judge the occasional lapse too harshly.

2. *Recognise the importance of attitude.* Numerous studies have demonstrated the effect of attitude on performance. You can control your attitude towards the situations in which you find yourself. Avoid any tendency to view yourself as unfortunate victim battered by circumstance. Instead, adopt the role of competent professional in control of the situation, approaching problems creatively and constructively in the knowledge that you can find a way through them.

3. *Shift your viewpoint.* There is always more than one perspective on a situation. It is quite possible to shift your viewpoint on events in order to give yourself a foothold for recovery. The way to do this is to question yourself:
   - How else can I look at this?
   - What are my options?
   - What new things have I learnt from this experience?
   - What can I do better next time?

Questions require answers that will guide you in the direction of a positive response to the difficulty. But they must be the right sort of questions – those that will carry you forward. Simply raking over the debris is not the way to do it. So don't ask 'Where did I go wrong?' (backward-looking). Reframe the question as 'What will I do differently in future?' (forward-looking).

4. *Set your own criteria for a job well done.* In the case study, Sarah was measuring her success entirely on the basis of feedback she hoped to receive from her audience. Receiving none, she judged herself to have failed. In effect, she was putting her self-confidence in the hands of others. Wherever possible make your measures of achievement independent of other people's judgement or your perceptions of their judgement. With a job interview, for example, step back from the result and look at how you dealt with the questions, not whether the selectors chose you. This approach not only frees you from over-reliance on the estimation of others, it gives you a lead into examining what you might do differently in future.

5. *Get it in proportion.* When you're in the middle of it, the sensation of failure feels like the most important thing in the world. But ask yourself how much it will matter in 10 years' time. Look back to previous occasions when you felt you had failed. Were they really as desperate as they seemed at the time? And what about the people who you think have witnessed your stupidity? Are they really judging you? Do you spend your time watching out for other people's blunders and recording them? Of course not. The chances are that even if you have made a fool of yourself, others will not have noticed or will have forgotten about it.

6. *Abandon the notion that the game is only worth playing if you win.* Of course you should aim for success and celebrate it, but if success is the only thing that matters then the pain and disappointment of setbacks will be much harder to bear. Concentrate on the process and not just the prize. Take satisfaction in getting the details of what you are doing right, and reward yourself for tackling obstacles that may be thrown in your path along the way.

7. *Don't take it personally.* One of the most common and unfortunate tendencies in dealing with setbacks and failure is to treat them not as challenges to change our behaviour, but as indicators that there is something wrong with us. We start to see ourselves as *failures* rather than *people who have experienced failure*. The ability to learn from failure is important, and learning will be hampered if failure is always accompanied by self-disparagement.

8. *Keep a record of setbacks overcome.* When you are confidently facing a new challenge, what is it that leads you to say 'I can handle this'? Generally it is experience. You remember dealing successfully with a previous problem that was in some way similar. There is a reference you can draw upon that leads you to believe that you can make a success of the new challenge. In Chapter 1 we looked at drawing up a list of achievements. You might like to take this a stage further by maintaining a diary in which you record challenges overcome and achievements, however small. Use it also to register the steps you will take to bounce back from setbacks and disappointments. Setting these things down on paper helps you to adopt a problem-solving approach and gives a sense of commitment. And at times of future difficulty you have a record that proves you are able to

build yourself back up from even the toughest of reverses.

9. *Laugh.* The ability to laugh at yourself is an essential skill of the survivor. Searching out the humour in your situation allows you to step back and get it into perspective. It has also been shown that laughter has a genuine role in the reduction of stress and tension. Many of us find it easy to look back on events and laugh, but feel it is somehow not proper to search out the humour at the time it will do us most good. When we laugh at ourselves we are acknowledging our shortcomings in a way that doesn't carry the negative impact of self-condemnation and puts us in a state of mind where we are ready to bounce back.

10. *Remember that overcoming failure is vital to achievement.* Some of the best-known achievements are only known to the world because their originators persisted in the face of failure. It is said that Thomas Edison made almost 2,000 attempts before he succeeded in producing a workable light bulb. Henry Ford reportedly went broke five times before he finally succeeded; and Winston Churchill only became Prime Minister at the age of 65 after a career marked by defeats and setbacks. All three had something to say on the subject of failure:

Many of life's failures are people who didn't realise how close they were to success when they gave up.

Thomas Edison

Failure is the opportunity to begin again more intelligently.

Henry Ford

Success consists of going from failure to failure without loss of enthusiasm.

Winston Churchill

handling disappointment

Everything that has been said so far cannot take away the fact that disappointment hurts. It doesn't have to result in self-condemnation, loss of confidence and giving up, but for all that it still stings. As with any injury it may need a bit of nursing, so don't expect that you will always be able to bounce back immediately. But the quicker you are on your feet the sooner you'll get over it, and the less chance there is of negative influences sapping your confidence. So give yourself a day or two, no more, before you start to turn things around.

dealing with mistakes

Only a fool would claim never to have made a mistake in his or her working life, but there is a natural tendency to shrink from revealing our mistakes. We fear the response we may receive – loss of status, ridicule, humiliation. But as even the most cursory study of political and corporate cover-ups in recent years will show, concealment uncovered inevitably does more damage than the original error.

Obviously you will seek to avoid making mistakes if possible, but the only sensible advice for dealing with them when they do occur is to be up-front about them straight away. Not only are you more likely to receive greater understanding and support than if a mistake leaks out at a later date, but so far as your own confidence is concerned, it helps you to recover and put the error behind you.

Here is a three-step approach to dealing with mistakes appropriately:

1. If the mistake is yours, acknowledge responsibility. Don't seek to shift the blame on to other people. There may be relevant contributory factors such as the long

hours you have been working or the fact that you didn't receive some information you needed, and it may be relevant to mention these, but don't use them as pillars to hide behind.

2. Indicate what you have learnt. Mistakes, like any other setbacks, should be opportunities for learning and your admission is likely to be more favourably received if you acknowledge this.

3. Show what you are doing to remedy the mistake and what you will do differently in future. This not only provides reassurance for your boss or your team, but also enables you to move on.

I need to acknowledge here the impact of organisational culture on the extent to which mistakes are acknowledged and used as learning opportunities. Many professions and organisations still have 'blame cultures' in which the primary concern is to bring the perpetrator of the error to book, and scant consideration is given to addressing systems and practices to reduce future occurrences of the same problem. Working in such an environment is confidence-sapping and does not encourage openness with regard to one's own errors. But, difficult though it may be, I would still maintain that openness is the best bet. Shifting a blame culture is not easy, but it can be done. It requires managers who are prepared not only to subscribe in principle to the notion that we all make mistakes and should be enabled to learn from them, but also to carry that commitment into day-to-day dealings with their colleagues.

Before we leave the subject of mistakes, let's briefly consider three further pointers that can help retain confidence.

eliminate negative messages

What sort of messages do you give yourself when you make an error? Routinely calling yourself an idiot or questioning your competence may seem harmless enough, but over time it can play a part in the erosion of self-worth. Be a little kinder to yourself. Without in any way denying the error, recognise that everyone makes mistakes, and it is much more valuable to learn lessons from them than to chastise yourself.

don't turn good decisions into mistakes

With hindsight it is often possible to realise that other courses of action would have been more appropriate. But that does not turn the decision made into a mistake. Circumstances may have changed for reasons you couldn't have predicted at the time of the decision. New information may have become available. Provided you weighed up the options and reached the conclusion you did on the basis of the best information available to you at the time, then the decision remains a good one. You may have to take action to recover from what has turned out not to be the best course of action, but don't beat yourself about the head with self-recrimination along the lines of 'I should have' and 'if only I had'.

strategic apologies

There are some occasions when it can pay to apologise for something that is neither your fault nor your responsibility. Such apologies used appropriately can be disarming and can swiftly take the heat out of pointless confrontation. Provided you are clear in your own mind about the reason for the apology – not unassertive behaviour on your part, but a gesture made to break a logjam – then you will come away from the situation with your confidence intact or even enhanced. But don't get into the habit of issuing such apologies just for an easy life. That is the mark of somebody asking to be walked upon.

overcoming fears and worries

fears

Ask anybody what they are afraid of and you're likely to be presented with a whole range of responses: heights; snakes; illness; flying, etc. Generally speaking we don't mind owning up to these. But unless you're a steeplejack or a zookeeper, these are not the fears that are likely to arise in a modern workplace. The most widespread workplace fears are social ones – fear of confrontation, fear of making a fool of oneself – and they are generally more difficult to acknowledge.

The way we most commonly respond to things that make us anxious or fearful is to avoid them. Avoidance takes various forms:

- procrastination – I'll deal with it tomorrow, next week, next month;
- using other tasks as distractions to prevent us having to face up to those we are afraid of;
- using other people as props or shields;
- bottling up our fears and not admitting them even to ourselves.

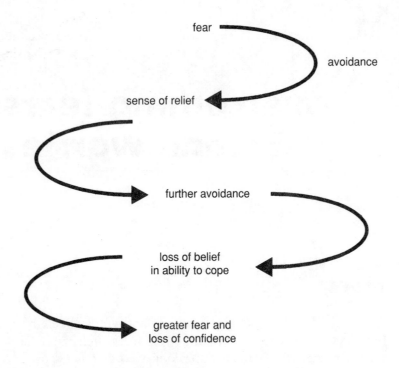

Figure 3.1 *Spiral of avoidance*

But the more we avoid those things that make us anxious, the greater the fear becomes. The initial avoidance eases our anxiety, which leads us to employ the same strategy next time the threatening situation presents itself. With each incidence of avoidance it becomes more difficult to face up to whatever we are afraid of and our confidence declines accordingly. We are locked into a vicious spiral of avoidance (see Figure 3.1).

Once we are into the spiral of avoidance it's easy for the fear to assume a level of importance quite disproportionate to the actual danger we face.

Avoidance may give us a temporary feeling of relief, but it does so at the expense of a longer-term decline in self-belief and, as if that were not bad enough, the niggling feeling that we should be doing something about it doesn't go away either. There is only one way to deal with fears and that is by facing up to them. All the time that we engage in avoidance activity we are telling ourselves that the pain of facing our fears will be greater than the pain of avoiding them. We need to reverse that situation and make the pain of *not* handling them greater than the pain of handling them.

Early in my career I used to be afraid of speaking up at meetings and conferences. The presenter would invite questions, hands would go up, but never mine. I was convinced that any question I asked would expose me as a complete idiot and subject me to the ridicule of all present. So I would sit there, mouth firmly closed, unasked questions locked inside my head. From time to time somebody would ask one of 'my' questions and I would notice other heads nodding around the room. Nobody laughed at the questioner, but then he probably expressed it better than I would have done. That's what I told myself anyway. It was a long time before I realised that I wasn't unique – that others, whose silence I took to be quiet confidence, were afflicted by just the same fear of making fools of themselves. That's the thing about fear: it exists just in your mind and is often invisible to others.

The time came when I couldn't bear sitting silent any longer. I opened my mouth and felt everyone's attention on me. A particularly strangled version of my voice seemed to come from a point about three feet behind my head, and made a point of such mind-boggling inanity that I was convinced everyone would fall about laughing. They didn't; the ceiling didn't fall in. One or two people might even have nodded. Sure, I felt a bit of an idiot, but not nearly as much of one as I had been in my fearful imaginings. And, of course, the next time I came to speak it was easier, and the next and so on.

how to tackle your fears

Standing up to your fears is not a matter of ability so much as motivation. They are your fears – you created them – and what you have made you can destroy.

So start by asking yourself some firm questions:

■ What is it I am avoiding?
■ Why am I avoiding it?
■ What have I gained by avoiding it?
■ What will I lose by not tackling it?
■ If I face up to this fear, what is the worst thing that can happen to me?
■ What will I gain by facing up to this fear?
■ How will I feel after I have faced up to it?
■ How will facing up to it help me the next time I have a similar challenge?

Answering such questions honestly will help you to deal with fears more rationally, and to reduce the element of disproportion that tends to come about when we allow them to rampage unchecked. But you may still need some further strategies if you are to swing the balance decisively in favour of tackling them. Here are six methods you may find useful:

1. **Graded challenges**
   Wherever it is possible to do so, adopt a gradual approach to confronting your fears. Jumping in at the deep end may help some people to swim, but it's more likely to terrify most to the point that they never want to go near the water again. So your first stage in facing up to a feared activity should be to set yourself a challenge that makes you anxious but isn't so scary

that you are unable to tackle it. If, as I was, you are scared of speaking up at meetings, then you might set yourself the target of just asking one question, or making one simple point. Reward yourself for achieving this, and stick with the same level of participation until you feel comfortable with it, and then raise the bar. Set yourself a new level, reward yourself, stick with it until comfortable and raise the bar again. It won't always be a constant upward curve. There will be setbacks and times when your confidence takes a dip, but provided you keep setting yourself achievable challenges and rewarding yourself immediately for overcoming them, the overall trend will be upwards.

2. **Visualisation**

Some of the challenges you may fear in your job are not amenable to the 'one step at a time' treatment. For example, if confrontation is an issue for you and you are faced with having to discipline a member of your team, then the sort of gradualist approach I have described above won't get you too far. You need to take the bull by the horns. In such circumstances visualisation techniques can be an extremely helpful way of preparing yourself for the encounter.

Visualisation is best known in the sports arena. All top athletes and sports people use a tactic of mental rehearsal in which they visualise themselves achieving the standards they are training for – running that bit faster, jumping that bit further and so on. There is no doubt that it works, and can apply equally to other forms of human endeavour. Routinely picturing yourself succeeding at whatever you set out to do can make a significant difference to your performance. It serves to remove psychological limitations you have placed on yourself through previous perceptions of failure and negative self-talk.

How to do it

Visualisation is most effective if you are relaxed when you do it, so you might want to go through a conscious relaxation routine before you start. Some people claim that it works best if practised just prior to a night's sleep, although if you normally experience difficulty shutting off your thoughts and falling asleep, it is best to avoid such timing. Once you are relaxed, you can put your imagination to work not only on the images of the event you seek to visualise, but on the associated words and feelings too.

Using the example I introduced at the start of this section – a tricky meeting at which you have to discipline a difficult member of your team – mentally rehearse the interview. Visualise the way you will talk to the person, the words you will use, even your confident body language. Picture yourself handling the situation successfully and assertively. Visualise the event not just as a sort of slide show, but as a dynamic enactment with you as the central participant. You remain relaxed and in control, breathing calm and regular, no hint of becoming angry or flustered. You are using the right words in the way that you would like to. Your body language demonstrates confidence and assurance. The mental rehearsal you give yourself by this activity can be almost as beneficial as actual experience, and can considerably reduce anxiety levels.

If possible, run a visualisation several times to make a real difference to performance. Don't let any negative elements come into the picture – if they do, gently let them go. Don't dwell on them or force them out. Remember that visualisation is a supplement to, not a replacement for, other preparation. You still need to do the normal work in preparation for whatever the challenge might be.

Visualisation is not only useful in facing up to your fears. You can use it to lift your performance in all manner of individual events and regular occurrences or as a way of maintaining motivation and reinforcing belief in your ability to reach longer-term goals.

3. **Affirmations**

    Our self-belief or absence of it is partly a result of messages we have fed ourselves. This is particularly the case with things that make you anxious or afraid. We indulge in negative self-talk – messages such as 'I'm never going to manage this. It's too scary. Might as well give up now.' But just as negative self-talk leads to loss of confidence, positive affirmations can boost it. Consciously eliminate the negative messages and replace them with simple constructive statements of encouragement. Repeated frequently enough they can make a real difference to your performance.

4. **Reverse the order**

    Arrange your list of things to do with those tasks you fear at the top of the list and the ones you enjoy most at the bottom. Tackle the list in order, and not only do you get the relief that comes from overcoming challenges that otherwise might have been postponed, but you are also rewarded with successively more attractive tasks as you work your way down the list.

5. **Immediacy**

    When you have resolved to tackle something that makes you anxious, get on with it as soon as possible. The longer you leave it, the more you will find yourself inventing excuses, allowing the fear to grow or re-establish itself. If you have decided to speak up at a meeting, say something early on, even if it is just to ask a question. Rather like the goalkeeper's early touch of the ball in a football match, it gives your confidence a lift that helps when you come to be more severely tested. Where the activity you fear is not one that you can deal with immediately, at least do something that commits you – arrange an appointment or schedule a time when you will deal with it.

6. **References**

   Remember how it felt when you did it. It is very important to hang on to the sense of relief and accomplishment that follows from successfully confronting a situation that made you anxious. Remember how different it feels from the temporary relief of avoidance. Note also how situations seldom turn out to be as difficult as you had feared. Log all these thoughts and feelings in your memory bank so you can draw on them if you are tempted to bottle out of a frightening situation in future.

Courage is very important. Like a muscle it is strengthened with use.

Ruth Gordon

worry

Worry is one of the primary ingredients in loss of confidence. Just think about the effects it has on us:

   ■ reduced ability to concentrate;
   ■ sense of being out of control;
   ■ wasted time and energy;
   ■ increased tension and fatigue;
   ■ difficulty making decisions;
   ■ feelings of fear and confusion.

Is there anything valuable about worry? Well, maybe. In so far as it acts as a spur to prepare us for action and allows us to plan and rehearse the way we will deal with a problem, worry is a normal and natural activity. The difficulty comes with a response that is out of proportion to the seriousness of the problem and where, in the jargon, we catastrophise, assuming the worst possible outcome and introducing all manner of irrational or unlikely possibilities. Some of us are natural worriers. If you are one you will know all about it. But few are immune from worry, and even the most insouciant among us may fall victim when under pressure.

combating worries

There is a variety of ways to reduce your tendency to worry. You can:

- prevent worries arising in the first place by the way you set about tackling problems;
- attack them with rational analysis;
- limit the occasions when you will permit them to occur;
- disperse them with imaging, mind calming and distraction.

You may find that some strategies work better for you than others. Experimentation will help, but don't expect a technique to work first time or every time you try it. Be prepared to ring the changes. To give you some choice, here are 10 approaches you might try:

1. **A systematic approach to problems**
    Worry is at its most acute in the period between awareness of a problem and a decision being taken. As concerns multiply, your ability actually to reach a decision is diminished. If you are able to adopt an approach that leads you swiftly and efficiently from problem to decision, you will greatly reduce the inci-

dence of worries running riot. This isn't to say that you should charge into decisions without adequate consideration, but neither should you paralyse yourself with over-analysis and dread of making the wrong move. There are several steps in the process:

a. *Outlining the problem*

How you define the problem will determine the solutions you arrive at, so take care to ensure you are tackling the real issue. Where the problem is a complex one, perhaps with several interwoven issues, there may be some unravelling to be done. Also be sure that you understand why it has arisen, and what the timescale is for resolving it.

b. *Identifying the available options*

Take time to clarify the courses of action open to you, but avoid overkill. Excessive information gathering and analysis will drive your worry level up. If you have difficulty identifying more than one or two options, a little brainstorming may be in order.

c. *Considering the pros and cons of each option*

A balance-sheet approach is a useful way to do this. Draw a line down the middle of a sheet of paper and, for each option, list the pros on one side and the cons on the other. But don't treat the pros and cons as if they all carry equal weight. A single point against may be of such weight that it eliminates all the points in favour. Beware also of what may seem to be overwhelming pros. The novelty value of some options may lead to the cons not being adequately explored.

d. *Selecting the best option*

This is where the potential for dithering is at its greatest. People who worry excessively feel they have to be absolutely sure that a decision is the right one before they are prepared to go ahead. But the mere fact that a problem is causing you worry means that there is unlikely to be a perfect solution. So it's a matter of choosing the best fit, taking account of the balance of risk against potential gain.

e. *Moving on*

Once the decision is taken you must move on. The worst of all worlds is to keep revisiting the issue and worrying over whether you made the right decision. Of course, you cannot expect to get it right all the time. When you take the decision its implementation lies in the future and circumstances may change. But arriving at the decision in a considered and systematic manner means that you are going to be right more often than not. Accept that the future is uncertain, make clear decisions and feel your confidence grow and your worries subside.

2. **Analysing your worries**

Get to grips with what it is you are really worrying about. Worry is often concerned with all sorts of vague and groundless fears that have acquired significance totally disproportionate to their likelihood of occurring. A good way to clarify and appraise your concerns is to write down what it is you are anticipating might happen and then turn your attention to verifying the likelihood of these forecasts actually coming about.

Divide a sheet of A4 into three columns. Label the left-hand column *Prediction*, the middle column *Grade* and the right-hand column *Worst Outcome*. The first column is for clarifying what you are worrying about. Break it down into the various things you are concerned might happen (see example on page 36).

In the middle column give each of these predictions a grade from zero to five depending on the likelihood of it actually happening:

0 = Unknown – with the information available at the present time you cannot possibly know if this

may happen. There may be further information to be acquired, or it may be a situation where only time will tell. Either way there is no point in worrying about it now.

1 = Impossible – this is a completely irrational worry; discard it.

2 = Highly unlikely – also one for the discard pile, unless you are concerned with an issue where there has to be a very high level of certainty.

3 = Possible.

4 = Probable.

5 = Certain.

In the third column indicate the worst thing that could happen if a prediction graded between three and five were to be realised.

Example

Terry has been unexpectedly offered a more responsible job with another company. He is worried about whether he should take it. He breaks down his concerns as follows:

Prediction	Grade	Worst Outcome
Something better may come along where I am now.	0 (unknown)	Can't know what the future will bring. Dismiss this concern.
The new firm may have a restructuring and, as the new boy, I would be the first to go.	3 (possible)	Need to look for another job, but could do so with the benefit of a more comprehensive CV.
This is a more responsible job. I may fail at it.	2 (highly unlikely)	I haven't failed at anything previously and I am handling current responsibilities easily. Dismiss this worry.
Further to travel each day. May find it too much hassle.	4 (probable)	May need to move house at some stage in the future, but that's not out of the question.

Setting your concerns out in this way allows you easily to discard the groundless worries, and to match those more likely to happen against the consequences if they do come about.

3. **Talking about them**

    Talking your worries through with someone else can be very helpful provided you pick the right person. Avoid the sort who will treat the discussion as an opportunity to tell you what you should do. Somebody else's instant solutions may feel initially comforting, but ultimately they won't do anything for your self-confidence. The most productive discussion will be with somebody who is able to ask questions that allow you to clarify your concerns and evaluate your options. An arrangement of mutual support, whereby colleagues effectively counsel each other through difficulties, offers a framework in which to achieve this.

4. **Applying the 10-year test**

    A useful way to scale down worries that have got out of hand is to ask yourself how much the consequence you are worried about will matter in 10 years' time. The usual answer is that it will hardly matter at all.

5. **Holding a worry audit**

    This is a useful technique to remind yourself how pointless most worry is:

    -   Make a list of the things you have worried about in the last year – or at least those you can remember.
    -   Ask yourself how many have actually happened.
    -   Of those that have come about, how many would have been worse if you hadn't worried about them?
    -   And how many could have been prevented if you had worried about them a bit more?

Sobering, isn't it? And how ironic that many of the real disasters in our lives are the ones that come out of the blue – the ones we wouldn't have thought to worry about.

6. **Allocating worry time**
    Some people find that they can limit their worries by postponing them to a designated 'worry time'. They allocate half an hour each day when they will permit themselves to worry, and any worries that pop up at other times of the day are postponed until that time. I have to admit that this approach hasn't worked for me, but then I'm the sort of impatient soul who likes to get on with things immediately, and that applies as much to worrying as to everything else. Fans of this approach suggest that if you can't manage to post-pone your worries until the designated time, you at least put them off for a few minutes. That way you reduce the sense of urgency and panic that is a frequent accompaniment to worrying.

7. **Drawing a line under the things you cannot influence**
    One of the most irritating and energy-sapping things about worry is that we carry on doing it when there is nothing we can do to influence or change events. It is optimistic to expect that you will ever be able to completely eliminate such thoughts from your mind, but you can downgrade their effect considerably by a conscious attempt at identification and relega-tion.

8. **Learning to live in the present**
    Worrying is an activity that tends to focus on the future – what might happen, what might go wrong. Planning and preparing for the future are very neces-sary activities, but if we are not careful we can find ourselves inhabiting a world of constant calculation, prediction and worry. Now is the only time we have in which to do our real living but, with our attention

elsewhere, we seldom get full value from the present moment. So, whenever you find your thoughts dwelling too frequently on the 'maybes' and the 'what ifs', make a conscious effort to focus on what is happening right now. Just experience it, don't try to think about it or analyse it. And allow no thoughts about past or future to intrude. For the busy-minded individual it's not easy to hold that focus for long. But keep working at it; you'll find that over time you are able to do it more easily.

9. **Imaging and mind calming**

Rational approaches are all very well, but in the middle of the night when worries crowd in, chasing one another in crazy spiral, reason seems like a fairly scarce commodity. In such circumstances many people find imaging techniques a helpful way of putting their worries to one side. You might, for example, picture yourself digging a deep hole, throwing your worries into it one by one and then filling in the hole again. Alternatively, try mentally parcelling your worries up and throwing them off a high building or into the sea.

The mind-calming influence of meditation can be tremendous help in dealing with serious and persistent worries. I am not able here to embark upon any serious consideration of it, but if you want to enjoy its benefits there are many excellent books and tapes available.

10. **Distraction**

Distraction is not to be confused with avoidance. If analysis suggests that there is something you can do about your worries and it is something you can get on with immediately, then that is what you should do. Distraction is the strategy to adopt when there is nothing that can be done in the immediate term and nothing to be gained by further analysis of your concerns. What you are essentially doing is to force out your worries by steering your attention into other unrelated activities. The best sorts of distraction activities are things that you find enjoyable and demanding to the extent that you are able to become immersed in them. You will know the sort of work tasks that fall into this category. Away from work, distraction might comprise any recreational activity, but those involving some physical exertion are particularly valuable in that they provide an outlet for tension. If there is a boredom factor in the alternative activity, you may find your thoughts harking back to the worries you're trying to leave behind, and the same may be the case if the activity is so demanding that you find it an effort to keep your full attention focused on it.

Don't worry that the world is coming to an end today. It's already tomorrow in Australia.

Charles Schultz

dealing with difficult people

Difficult people present some of the most confidence-sapping of workplace experiences. In addition to anger and frustration, they can lead you to doubt your abilities as a manager, supervisor or team colleague. People relationships are complex and I would not want to present pat solutions to dealing with difficult characters. But there are some general principles that, with an element of judgement on your part, should help to make life easier.

people who are always difficult

Some people fall into a group that I will call the perennially awkward. These are the real professionals. They have been the way they are for as long as anyone can remember and they are difficult with everybody. Here are three examples:

- Jane is a martyr. She believes that she is exploited, taken for granted and generally put upon, and she misses no opportunity to tell people about it. To her manager she appears to wallow in her misfortune. He is concerned that her gloomy nature is starting to have an effect on the morale of other members of the team.

■ Keith is a buck-passer. He is adept at getting other people to take on responsibility for tasks that should rightfully be his. His manager and colleagues are in despair at the frequency with which he succeeds by a mixture of flattery, feigned incompetence and deviousness to dump his problem work on to them. Of course, when things go wrong he is equally adept at shifting the blame.

■ Andrew is a tinpot dictator. He is fiercely protective of his area of responsibility and regards himself as constantly under threat of invasion. He reacts to any perceived incursion of his territory with immediate aggression, often flying into quite frightening rages. If unable to get his own way by direct attack he will resort to any other means at his disposal, including stabbing his perceived opponent in the back. He is unable to function as a team player and neither trusts nor is trusted by anyone, but much to the annoyance of those who have to continue trying to work with him, he is technically highly competent.

people who become difficult

By no means all the difficult people we encounter at work are drawn from the ranks of the perennially awkward. There may be others among your colleagues who are selectively difficult – experiencing clashes with certain individuals or responding negatively to particular events. People become difficult because of things that happen to them or perceptions they form about others.

For a number of years Derek worked as number two in a department headed by Barry, an ineffective manager close to retirement. Derek was regarded by most people as the *de facto* head, and was the one to whom people turned in respect of all the important issues. When Barry retired, Derek expected to get the job, and was shocked when Chris, an external candidate, was appointed. Chris was full of energy and ideas, and keen to make his mark on the department. Derek felt he was no longer being listened to. His confidence took a dive and he responded by becoming increasingly difficult and moody. Chris was puzzled and irritated by his behaviour, but neither man took any steps to resolve the relationship difficulties. As time went on, Chris turned to others to fulfil the responsibilities that Derek had previously held. Derek, his skills and experience overlooked, lost touch still further and became increasingly bitter. Eventually his post was declared redundant and he took a lower-paid and less responsible job in another company.

Similar scenarios are played out in workplaces everywhere. In this instance, Derek and Chris both felt the other to be difficult and unreasonable. The problems between them grew, with no attempt at resolution, and both men suffered. It might seem that Derek was the sole victim, but Chris had the aggravation associated with working around a non-functioning member of staff, and was denied the benefit of Derek's experience amassed over a number of years.

There are all sorts of reasons why people may become difficult:

■ They are angry about something you have done or they think you have done.
■ They are feeling insecure and lacking confidence.
■ They think you are trying to get one over on them.
■ Somebody else has upset them.
■ Something outside the work setting is bugging them.
■ They think you are not listening to them.

courses of action

Whether dealing with a member of the awkward squad or someone with whom we have had a specific problem, there are three basic courses of action open to us. We can ignore the problem, seek to avoid the person or to confront the issue. Unfortunately, many of us have a tendency to take a line that skirts all three. We shrink from confronting the behaviour directly, but demonstrate our hostility towards the person by indirect means:

■ sarcasm and put-downs;
■ seeking to ostracise the person, maintaining a hostile silence;
■ reciprocal behaviour – mirroring the treatment we believe the person is giving us;
■ explosions – blowing up over minor or unrelated issues;
■ running the person down to others.

This sort of guerrilla warfare can rumble on for years, escalating the conflict way beyond the original perceived injury. To spare ourselves the debilitating effects of ongoing friction, it's important to decide as early as possible whether to confront the problem behaviour or to refuse to be bothered by it and to accept the person as he or she is.

First consider the effect of the person's behaviour.

Ask yourself:

■ Is it preventing me from doing my job properly? ☐
■ Is it detrimental to the work of the team? ☐
■ Is it limiting the effectiveness of anybody for whose work I am responsible? ☐
■ Is it presenting an unfavourable impression to clients or other people whose views may have an impact on our continuing success? ☐

If the answer to all these questions is no, then you are only victimising yourself if you continue to be upset by the behaviour. Hanging on to resentment will hurt you more than it does the other person. People will always do things that have the potential to irritate you. It is up to you whether you let them get to you. You may need to work at desensitising yourself. Identify the behaviour that normally triggers a negative reaction from you and visualise yourself responding with calm good humour. Give yourself positive affirmations – 'I am in control of my responses' – and recognise the confidence-boosting effect that comes from greater ability to let the minor irritations of others wash over you.

I'm not suggesting here that you should put up with behaviour that is abusive or has a negative effect on your work or that of others for whom you are responsible. In such circumstances action is called for, and generally the sooner you take it the better.

confronting problem behaviour

When you decide to confront problem behaviour, it helps greatly to be clear about the results you are seeking. You wish the person to be aware of his or her behaviour and its consequences, but your primary objective should be to resolve the problem rather than to lay blame. Remember that in the eyes of the other person you may be the difficult one. In all probability the person is chugging along convinced of the rightness of his or her actions, so coming at him or her in commando or lecturing mode is unlikely to be productive. You should neither expect nor try to change personality, but provided you go about it in the right way you can influence attitudes and modify behaviour. If you want to be successful, you need to give attention to when, where and how you deal with the issue.

choosing the time and place

Although it may seem sensible to wait for a suitable time when you can drop an issue naturally into the conversation, it is not necessarily a wise or easy thing to do. Many of us have a fundamental dislike of confrontation and will tend to shy away from grasping the moment when it occurs. We have understandable fears about what the person's reaction may be – concern about a temperamental outburst or retaliation – and the prospect of addressing an issue face to face may appear harder to bear than the constant drip of poor working relationships. We tell ourselves that the next time the problem surfaces we will do something about it, but when you have postponed action a couple of times it is easy to procrastinate endlessly. Even discounting this tendency, an approach that relies on seizing the moment has other drawbacks:

- ▓ You will invariably be raising the matter alongside other issues and this may dilute the importance of what you are trying to say.
- ▓ The moment is likely to be fleeting; you will not have much opportunity to collect your thoughts in advance.
- ▓ The other person may interpret an issue raised in passing as being of only minor significance.
- ▓ You may find yourself raising the issue at a time when you are angry about something else and allowing your emotions to get in the way of what you are trying to say.
- ▓ Opportunities to raise the problem may only occur in unfavourable settings, for example when others are present.

If an issue is worth raising, it's worth giving it a proper time slot. How you go about this will depend on your relationship with the person with whom you need to discuss the problem.

raising problems with your boss

If you have a regular one-to-one meeting this should be the time to raise the problem. In the absence of a regular session, or if your boss is the type who treats such occasions as opportunities to listen to his or her own voice, you may need to ask for a specific session to discuss the issue. Naturally, this will require a little diplomacy. Try to phrase your request in a manner that offers mutual advantage, for example 'I'd like to discuss ways in which we might work together more productively.'

raising problems with a colleague at the same level

Again it is generally best to seek a meeting when you can start to iron out the difficulty. Your opening request, 'I wonder if we could arrange to meet for 15 minutes this week to discuss an issue that's been bothering me,' might well draw the response 'Oh really, what's that?' Try to resist the temptation to be drawn into discussion of the issue there and then. Say something like 'I'd rather talk about it when we meet if that's OK.'

raising problems with a member of your team

Where you are the one in a position of seniority you have greater opportunity to determine how and when the problem will be aired. There are a lot of benefits in having a regular review session with your team members. Approached in an open way it will give you the chance to nip any interpersonal problems in the bud and to gain invaluable feedback on your own performance.

dealing with problems in an assertive manner

Handling difficult people assertively means:

▓ removing as far as possible any anger or tension from the meeting;

■ maintaining a polite but firm stance;
■ attempting to get on the other person's wavelength and understand his or her point of view;
■ recognising that your aim is not to point fingers, but to determine what you can do to improve the situation;
■ demonstrating a willingness to listen;
■ having an expectation of an open and courteous response.

before you meet

Think in advance about what you are going to say and how you are going to say it. Go over in your mind the words you will use to introduce the problem. Visualise yourself talking to the other person in a calm but assertive manner along the lines we discussed in the previous chapter.

when you meet

■ Introduce the problem clearly and calmly.
■ Avoid using emotive language and don't let yourself get angry, but let the other person know how his or her behaviour has made you feel.
■ Make it clear that you are not attacking the person's worth as a colleague. It is just this particular behaviour that is the problem.
■ Don't lecture. Present the problem as something that is causing difficulty for you both, and which you hope to be able to work out together.
■ Indicate that you are ready to listen to the person's response.
■ Actively listen to what the person has to say.
■ Take care to look forward in your expectations of the person. Excessively raking over what he or she should have done is not going to help either of you to move ahead.

You might be tempted to sugar the pill by telling the person the things you value about him or her – strengths, contribution to the organisation, etc. This may have some value as a way of introducing what you have to say, but beware of giving mixed messages. In the desire to avoid possible offence, it is easy to go over the top on the pluses to the detriment of what is important.

recognising that it isn't all the other person

Interpersonal problems are seldom entirely the fault of one person. If you are to make real progress in ironing out difficulties, it's important that you are able to recognise the other person's point of view, and be prepared to make some changes in your own approach. It isn't easy to do this. We commonly boost our own self-esteem by focusing on the mistakes of others; fail to see the interpersonal errors we make ourselves; and have difficulty understanding people whose thought processes and behaviour are different to our own.

Seeing the other person's point of view and being prepared to respond to it does not mean denying your own point of view or placing your self-confidence at the other person's mercy. If you are prepared to seek win/win solutions in an assertive manner you will generally enjoy greater respect from your colleagues than if you seek to protect your position at all costs.

varying your approach

The basic, calm, assertive approach outlined above will apply in all cases, but you will find it helpful to give some thought to shifting your emphasis depending on the sort of person you are dealing with. Returning for a moment to the examples I used at the start of this chapter: with martyrs the emphasis should be firmly on listening. They are people whose sense of grievance is fuelled by the perception that they are ignored. Show that you are prepared to hear the tale of woe without necessarily agreeing with it. Help them to identify options for change, but make sure it is they, and not you, who commit to taking action. With aggressive types the emphasis will be on de-escalating hostility. You will want to ensure that you do not let them intimidate you or goad you into retaliation.

Raising problems with difficult bosses can be extremely tricky. They have much more scope for unreasonable behaviour than peers or team members. You may need to convince them that ideas for change have originated from them, and to take care not to make them feel threatened. Try to work from their point of view and be prepared to credit them with motives they may not, in fact, possess. The important thing is that you achieve a change of behaviour, not that you score a victory.

influencing behaviour change

The manager who simply chews off a team member about his or her behaviour and expects immediate change is likely to be disappointed. Certainly there may be a grudging compliance in the face of threatened negative sanctions, but influencing change through positive reinforcement is a great deal more powerful. Positive reinforcement can be anything that increases the future frequency of a particular behaviour, and it works best if it follows that behaviour immediately and is specifically directed at the individual. It follows from this that waiting until the next appraisal meeting before you praise an individual for a change of behaviour, or making some positive general comments at a team meeting, will not do the trick.

You should look for even the smallest examples of behaviour changes and reinforce them immediately. This reinforcement may consist simply of letting the person know that you have noticed the change and offering a few words of encouragement. The effect of such modest measures can be remarkable.

Continue to look for successive changes and reinforce them in ways that the person will value – a demonstration of increased trust, perhaps, or a prized assignment. Positive reinforcement is not just something that applies between manager and team member. It works upwards, downwards and sideways.

Don't expect immediate results. You may need to work on tiny improvements for quite a while. But be prepared to keep going, deliver on your side of any deal and let the other person be aware that your expectations of them are unchanged.

establishing supportive relationships

Several times in this book I have written of the need to free yourself from over-reliance on the approval of others in the maintenance of your confidence. All of that stands, but seeking to foster mutually supportive workplace relationships takes nothing away in terms of self-reliance, and brings a number of additional benefits:

- There are bound to be times when your resolve dips. Other people can help you through those occasions, as you help them when they are feeling down.
- Colleagues can offer a valuable sounding board to help you articulate and examine ideas, fears, worries and solutions to problems.
- Supportive working relationships are pleasanter and more productive.

To obtain these benefits, you need to interact comfortably and openly, without being either overly dependent or too detached. Achieving that happy state requires:

- trust;
- flexibility;
- understanding of differences;
- realistic expectations;
- the ability to listen;
- the ability to give and receive feedback.

Building relationships is quite clearly a two-way process, but the only behaviour you can realistically work upon is your own. Other people will adjust their behaviour in response to you, but you cannot just expect them to change. So let's look at what you can do to develop and maintain supportive relationships.

building trust

When you trust somebody, you hold the belief that he or she won't exploit, cheat or use you in any way. You can rely on trusted people to do what they say they are going to do. You can share information in the knowledge that it will not be misused. Trust is the cornerstone of interpersonal relationships. A workplace in which there is a high level of trust is one where colleagues can feel secure and where genuine teamwork and co-operation can flourish. On the other hand, mistrust creates uncertainty, conflict and reduced individual confidence. Trust is a fragile thing. It can take a long time to build and a moment to destroy, and often it is the small things that knock holes in our trust.

activity

- Can you think of occasions in the past two years when your trust in others has been damaged?
- What were the behaviours that caused the damage?

The degree of trust in your workplace may depend to a significant extent on the culture of the organisation and the styles of its leaders. But even in an organisation characterised by internal competition and mistrust, it is still possible, and certainly desirable, to build and maintain high levels of trust with the people who comprise your immediate team or most regular contacts. Think about the different sorts of working relationships you have. In simple terms we might see them as falling into three levels:

1. *Nodding terms.* You exchange routine non-contentious information, make requests and deliver services as necessary.
2. *Constructive.* You are able to share information necessary for mutually effective performance, give and receive feedback, disagree without acrimony and rely upon professional levels of support and assistance.
3. *Close.* You are able to talk about worries and fears, and seek help and reassurance at any time.

As we develop relationships we generally progress through these levels a step at a time. At each step we venture a little more of ourselves and look to see if our trust is reciprocated. Some people find it hard to take even small risks in this way and remain distant and suspicious. A few leap in at an inappropriately advanced level. If you have ever had dealings with a person who comes in at level three you will know how alarming it can be to have a stranger suddenly presenting you with their innermost thoughts. It is unlikely to win your immediate trust. Indeed, it may have the contrary effect.

It isn't necessary for all your working relationships to reach that third level of closeness. Level two is perfectly adequate for a constructive working relationship. For those people who only figure marginally or occasionally in your working life, it may not be necessary to go beyond level one. But it is valuable to have at least one or two people with whom you can share anything that is bothering you.

Your personality, those of your colleagues, and the general working environment will influence to a significant extent the level of closeness you are prepared to contemplate. But if you are a manager or supervisor don't justify distant relationships with your staff on the basis that they are necessary to ensure adequate respect for your authority. That's garbage. While over-familiarity may be a mistake – the manager who attempts to be everyone's best friend is destined to come unstuck – it is not only possible but desirable to maintain a constructive working relationship with all members of your team, and to do so with no diminution of authority.

10 trust building blocks

1. *Trust others.* People respond when they feel them-selves to be trusted. That may seem obvious but it's remarkable how often it is overlooked, and how easy it is, even when you are trying to demonstrate trust, to get it wrong. We show trust not only by our words but by our actions, and it is common for the one to conflict with the other.

Linda delegates a responsibility to her assistant Caroline. She briefs Caroline thoroughly, sets clear objectives and gives her the necessary authority to act, stressing that Caroline enjoys her complete trust. So far, so good. But then as time goes on she cannot resist interfering. Although Caroline is delivering perfectly acceptable results, Linda shows her irritation that the job is being done differently to the way she previously tackled it. It is clear that she hasn't fully reconciled herself to passing over the responsi-bility, and her actions belie her earlier words.

2. *Be honest and direct.* Honesty and directness are not always popular, but people know where they stand with you and that will earn trust and respect. The honest colleague will give valuable, if sometimes uncomfortable, feedback and will feel able to express disagreement when need be. But for 'honest and direct' do not read 'blunt and aggressive'. Too many workplace thugs try to present their aggression as honesty. Don't buy it. You can be honest and direct but still compassionate and sensitive to the needs and rights of others. At the other end of the scale from the workplace thug is the chameleon who tries too hard to be liked by everyone. Chameleons alter their views depending upon whom they are talking to and always try to tell people what they think they want to hear. Such conduct may bring initial popularity, but in time colleagues may start to see through them and mistrust may develop.

3. *Be reliable.* Once we have been let down it's an uphill struggle to rebuild trust in the perpetrator. So don't make promises you can't keep and make sure that your reliability extends to small things as well as large.

4. *Be accountable.* Be prepared to take responsibility for mistakes without attempting to shift the blame on to others.

5. *Make consultation genuine.* People respond to being involved and consulted about decisions. But consultation that is just for the sake of appearances is worse than no consultation at all.

6. *Share praise.* Don't take all the credit for achievements that have resulted from a team effort. Make sure that team members are given immediate recognition and encouragement for the things they have done well.

7. *Remain accessible.* This doesn't mean putting up with every conceivable interruption at any time of the day. It is much more about an approachable attitude, interest and concern for the other members of your team and a readiness to listen.

8. *Don't blame.* Recognise that if progress is to be made then there are bound to be mistakes from time to time. Help your colleagues to learn from these and develop effective strategies for the future. It will result in greater productivity as well as increased trust.

9. *Share information.* Take a line on information that respects confidentiality while not harbouring information that should be exchanged. People who hang on to information to enhance their power may gain an advantage, but they won't win trust. Any instances of lack of openness that come to light are likely to give rise to the assumption that the person concerned engages in habitual concealment.

10. *Don't gossip.* People who talk about others behind their backs are seldom trusted. Even if the information does not find its way back to the subject, those who listen to the gossip may wonder whether they are to be the next victim.

activity

■ Are there people with whom you would like to have a closer, more trusting relationship?
■ What will you do to bring that about?
■ Has there ever been an indication that a colleague or colleagues don't trust you?
■ How might you be able to discover whether this is the case, and if it is, how important is it to you?
■ What might you be able to do to rebuild that trust?

being let down

It's not nice when you are let down, manipulated or rejected. But trust always involves some risk, and risks do not always pay off. If we are not prepared to take a risk with people then we will not form any worthwhile relationships, and we will seldom be surprised and delighted by them. Of course, it never makes sense to take stupid risks and there are some people who, regrettably, cannot be trusted. But the letdown always comes hardest when it is from a surprising quarter. On such occasions, rather than retiring to lick your wounds and vowing never to trust that person again, dust yourself off and assess the damage:

- ▨ Apart from bruised feelings, am I really any worse off? ☐
- ▨ Have I understood the situation correctly? Are there reasons for the other person's behaviour that I have missed? ☐
- ▨ Is it possible that I have jumped to conclusions? ☐
- ▨ Is there possible value in talking about it to the person concerned? ☐

Talking to the person is generally worth doing, unless it is a minor matter where you might risk making a mountain out of a molehill. But be sure that you approach the discussion in the right frame of mind. Follow the guidance in Chapter 4 on confronting problem behaviour.

The quality of Maggie's work has suffered a sudden and notice-able decline and her manager, Alison, asks her in to have a confidential chat about it. Maggie acknowledges that there is a problem, but reveals that it lies not at work but with difficulties in her marriage. Alison agrees to keep this information confidential and they agree upon ways in which she might help Maggie through a difficult patch. Maggie feels relieved that she has been able to talk about the problem and grateful for the offer of help. However, later that day one of her office colleagues makes a remark about marital difficulties. Maggie is horrified, convinced that Alison must have talked to others about her problems. The incident destroys her trust in Alison and causes her to withdraw even more into her shell.

You won't be surprised to learn that Maggie's trust hadn't been breached at all. The remark made by the other person was pure coincidence but, with her heightened sensitivity, Maggie assumed a link that wasn't there. Misconceptions like this happen all the time. You can probably think of examples in your own experience. And so often they are never cleared up.

flexibility

Good working relationships are like bridges: if they don't allow for some movement then they collapse. The person who always has to be right or always has to come out a winner will not be too successful. You need to know when to overlook failings and when to accept less than you might have been seeking. That doesn't mean you always have to compromise your own views or wind up with solutions that merely represent the least unattractive options. But you should ensure that other people's needs and points of view are fully taken into account and that decisions are not dictated by ego.

understanding differences

In our private lives we are able to seek out friends and partners whose personalities, interests and views correspond with our own, but at work there is a greater likelihood of finding ourselves bound together with people of a different outlook. However, the fact that people look at life from wholly different perspectives does not have to be a reason for gnashing of teeth. Handled properly it can be a team strength. So celebrate diversity, play to people's strengths and never assume you know what others are thinking.

Expectations of others should abide by the same conditions as those you set for yourself. They should be realistic and achievable, recognising that mistakes happen from time to time. People will tend to perform to your expectations of them. Value them and expect a positive contribution and you will generally be rewarded. Treat them as useless and lazy, and standards are unlikely to be high.

listening

The ability to listen is a skill we take for granted. Surely we need no training in something so basic. But we do. It's a talent that needs to be worked upon and one that, in our busy and impatient world, is often overlooked. We are inclined to regard it as a passive process, the same as hearing. But it shouldn't be so. Being able to listen actively and empathically is vital if we are to succeed in the resolution of interpersonal difficulties or help others find solutions to problems.

We have all met bad listeners. There are the people who are so busy thinking about how they will respond when you've finished that they don't pay attention to what you are saying at all. And then there are those awful individuals who like to demonstrate how tuned in to you they are by supplying the endings for your words and sentences. But for all that these types are a universal source of irritation, there is a bit of them in most of us. We mentally rush ahead, analysing what is being said, making judgements and assumptions, interrupting with our own thoughts and experiences.

There are four basic rules for effective listening:

1. *Give people time.* It is a rare individual who can accurately and cogently articulate his or her thoughts at the first take. And when the subject matter is to do with interpersonal difficulties or deeply felt problems it is especially hard. People need time to get their thoughts together. Listeners who jump in too quickly deny them that opportunity. Don't be afraid of silences – too often we leap to fill them and cut off a valuable train of thought in the process.

2. *Suspend judgement while you are listening.* At this stage it is unimportant whether you agree or disagree with what is being said. Signalling disagreement, for example, may lead to the speaker taking up a defensive position, which they will subsequently find it difficult to step away from. It's by no means easy to suspend judgement, especially if you have approached the discussion with strong views of your own. But work at it. It is important.

3. *Reflect back.* When the other person has finished making his or her point, summarise what you think has been said. This allows you to confirm the accuracy of your understanding, and also gives the other person the opportunity to correct anything not expressed accurately first time around. In reflecting back, it is important again to exclude judgements or assumptions of your own about what the person has said.

4. *Question.* If there are points of vagueness or uncertainty, encourage clarification by asking questions. Open questions – those that cannot receive a yes/no

answer – are most appropriate when you want to draw out further information without injecting your own assumptions or closing the discussion down on to one option. So rather than asking 'Do you want me to give you additional time with this project?' (closed question), ask 'What can I do that will enable you to complete this project?' (open question). Closed questions may be appropriate as follow-ups when you are narrowing down options.

What if you are dealing with a difference of opinion? 'Surely', you may say, 'I don't have to sit and listen to everything the other person has to say without indicating my own opinion or my disagreement at any stage.' Yes, you do, at least if you want to resolve the problem successfully. If you can demonstrate that you are able to listen, really listen, while the other person articulates his or her perception of the truth, and that you are prepared to do so without anger or judgement, you have a much greater chance of reaching an amicable solution. Of course, the other person must respect your right to be heard in the same way. There is a much greater chance of that happening if you have clearly set out the ground rules for the discussion in advance and stuck by them. Your introduction might be along the lines of 'I am going to listen to what you have to say as carefully as I can, and make sure that I understand your point of view. I hope that you will then do the same thing for me.'

maintaining relationships

Relationships, once established, need to be nurtured and maintained. It's easy to start taking colleagues for granted. At times of stress it will often be your best players, the ones you know you can rely upon, who are ignored. Maintaining an effective working relationship means taking time and trouble as part of your normal daily interactions. If you are a manager or supervisor, it is not sufficient to wait for the annual appraisal meeting to come around. Be alive to your team members' needs as well as your own. Look for things on which you can give positive feedback – even your star performers need it. Maintain a genuine interest in what they are doing and always remain accessible.

handling criticism and feedback

What happens when somebody criticises you? Do you:

- counter-attack by raising the other person's own short-comings?
- make flippant remarks?
- feel like bursting into tears?
- go away and sulk?

These are just a few of many common reactions to an experience that nobody finds entirely comfortable. They are all defensive responses, which have their roots in low self-esteem.

Everybody gets criticised at some time. It may arise from the most caring and constructive of motives – concern for our well-being, desire to help us change some perceived ineffective behaviour. Alternatively, it may be governed by vindictiveness and negativity – jealousy, anger, feelings of inferiority. Constructive criticism aims to change your behaviour. With destructive criticism the target is you.

Unfortunately, our initial response to both sorts is the same. We behave as if we are under attack – inappropriately, of course, because, until we have listened to and analysed what is being said, we do not know whether what we are experiencing is an attack or a favour. There are four less-than-satisfactory ways of dealing with criticism. We can ignore it, throw it back, deflect it or be defeated by it:

1. **Ignoring it**

   'I've spoken to him numerous times, and it's like water off a duck's back.' People who habitually ignore criticism protect themselves at the cost of never learning from others or changing their behaviour. They are locked into the rightness of their own points of view and regard criticism as misguided at best, treachery at worst. The ability to ignore criticism has its place. If you can identify and turn off the 'dripping taps' in your workplace and those inveterate critics who are just in the game of boosting their own self-image, then you can save yourself a lot of needless hassle. But don't seek to ignore as a sole strategy.

2. **Throwing it back**

   The urge to counter-attack is most prevalent when:
   - we are aware that we have made a mistake and are already mentally chastising ourselves;
   - we are feeling bruised;
   - the criticism is accompanied by attack on character or an attempt to label us – 'you're lazy, thoughtless', etc.

   Counter-attacking is seldom productive. While it might make you feel better briefly, the anger and emotion that goes into the response is likely to fuel longer-term resentment as well as escalating criticism into full-scale hostility and preventing you from hearing things that could be useful. Counter-attackers tend to make a habit of it regardless of the validity of the criticism or the scale of the problem.

3. **Deflecting it**

   This is almost the same as throwing it back. The

deflector uses flippancy to dilute the impact of what is being said or seeks to attribute blame elsewhere. To see this sort of thing in action you only have to watch parliamentary exchanges – sometimes entertaining, sometimes amusing, but seldom taking issues forward in any positive way.

4. **Being defeated by it**
   People who are defeated by criticism take the view that others know best and that what is being said simply confirms their uselessness. They take it all as comment on their very existence and are unable to distinguish between the constructive and the malicious.

receiving criticism confidently

The first step in handling criticism in a confident manner is to remove the notion that it represents an attack on all that you stand for. While that assumption is in place you are likely to react inappropriately. Certainly, some criticism will be unjustified or vindictive, but you can only judge its validity by listening dispassionately and removing anger and emotion from your response. If you can do this, you will be in a better position to respond assertively to negative criticism and to draw the useful lessons from constructive criticism.

calm down

The sense of being under attack invokes what is often referred to as the 'fight or flight' response. This involuntary primitive reaction stems from a time when threats were inevitably of a physical nature and the options for us were either to turn and confront the aggressor or scamper to the nearest tree. The body prepares itself for action by releasing hormones and by an increase in heart rate and blood pressure, rapid shallow breathing and increased perspiration. But the prospect of a physical response to a verbal attack is clearly inappropriate (I hope) in a modern workplace. Rather than a rapid physical response we need a calm rational one.

So when you feel yourself, literally, getting hot under the collar, what can you do to restore your cool? As I have said the symptoms of 'flight or fight' are involuntary, but the one you can control is breathing. Measured deep breathing really does work to restore balance and calm to your body and mind. Take a long, slow, deep breath, hold it to the mental count of four without straining, and release it in another long, slow breath. Pause for the mental count of four before taking the next inhalation. Continue with this regular deep breathing for as long as it takes for the symptoms to subside.

listen

The principles of active listening were covered in Chapter 5 but to reiterate, you need to:

- recognise that the other person has the right to a point of view;
- suspend judgement while the other person is talking – don't assume hostile motives;
- reflect back what you believe the person has said to confirm understanding – this is particularly necessary when receiving criticism as the anxiety that comes from feeling under attack can prevent you from accurately hearing what is being said;
- ask questions where necessary for clarification.

be objective

Try to step outside your feelings and view what is being said dispassionately. You may find it helpful to use a bit of imagery here. View the criticism as a parcel that is separate from either yourself or the critic. Your task is to decide whether it's a present or a bundle of garbage.

ask questions

Questions offer the most effective strategy for dealing with criticism:

- They allow you to appear reasonable, measured and in control even though you may be seething inside.
- They give you time to cool down. You're less likely to blow your top while you are concentrating on asking questions.
- Asking your critic to give more specific information allows you to ascertain whether there is any substance to complaints that are couched in generalities.
- Questions may help you to understand your critic's motivation better. Is he or she attempting to be genuinely constructive, or is there an element of jealousy or vindictiveness behind the remarks?
- You can put the ball back in the critic's court by asking what suggestions he or she has to resolve the matter.

Questions are a less inflammatory way of getting to the truth than direct challenges. Where it emerges that the critic is mistaken then that person is able to back down more easily than if, for example, you had called him or her a liar. The same applies if you are subsequently shown to be wrong.

seek a second opinion

If you are unsure whether a criticism is justified, seek a second opinion. Go to someone whose opinion you respect and try to approach him or her in a spirit of genuine enquiry, not defensiveness.

call time out

If you are feeling sensitive and vulnerable and are tempted to counter-attack, it can help to seek a postponement of the discussion rather than risk it descending into negativity. Be honest with the person making the criticism – 'I'll welcome hearing what you have to say, but I'm not feeling totally positive right now. Could we talk about it tomorrow?' Don't use this as a technique to put off criticism indefinitely. When you return to it, follow the principles on seeking feedback at the end of this chapter.

responding

So, you've managed to separate the accurate from the inaccurate, the constructive from the destructive. How do you respond?

If the criticism is accurate and constructive:

▓ acknowledge and accept it with good grace;
▓ make any apologies that may be necessary;
▓ tell the other person what you are going to do to resolve the situation.

If the criticism is accurate but destructive or vindictive:

▓ acknowledge any mistake you have made and apologise if necessary;
▓ respond assertively to destructive or vindictive comments;
▓ take whatever steps are necessary to remedy the situation.

If you believe the criticism is inaccurate:

▓ ask questions to determine how the misperception may

have arisen, and whether it is yours or the other person's;

▓ seek a second opinion if you are uncertain whether the criticism is accurate;

▓ correct any misperceptions.

If the criticism is both inaccurate and vindictive:

▓ remain calm;

▓ ask questions rather than making direct challenges;

▓ correct inaccuracies and respond to personal comments assertively;

▓ resist the urge to counter-attack;

▓ forget about the criticism.

Remember that even the most successful, competent and assertive people attract criticism. Use it as a tool for your own development, never as a catalyst for feuds and loss of confidence. Be reasonable, but never so reasonable that you neglect your responsibility to yourself.

feedback

The word 'feedback' is often used when information has been invited by the receiver and it may include an element of praise not present in much of what we refer to as criticism. But to a large extent the differences between criticism and feedback are more about perception than content. If we are the ones giving it or we like what we hear, we are more inclined to refer to it as feedback. However, regardless of the term you use, all the dangers of misperception and defensiveness are still present.

giving feedback

We perhaps need to remind ourselves why we are doing it. It is to make the other person aware of some aspect of his or her behaviour so that he or she may either change it or, in the case of feedback that comes in the form of praise, repeat it. It is not, or should not be, a form of revenge – a way of emphasising our superiority or an opportunity to score points. It is as well, therefore, to refrain from offering feedback when you are angry or irritated by the person in question.

Giving feedback is not always a comfortable thing to do. A common reason is anxiety about the other person's reaction. Will what we say hurt the person's feelings? Will he or she be angry? We may have additional concerns about the validity of our judgement or our ability to get the message across. As a consequence, openings for valuable and constructive feedback are often ducked or dealt with in a manner that is less than helpful. Even giving positive feedback on a job well done is not always easy. Many people find it difficult to express praise, and either dodge the opportunity entirely or overcome their embarrassment by combining praise with less complimentary remarks.

Let's look at handling it well.

if the other person has asked for feedback

Feedback that has been requested is easier to embark upon than feedback that you may be volunteering unasked. But unless you are absolutely clear about what you want to say, resist responding to a request until you have had time to collect your thoughts. A useful way of giving yourself time, and also of defusing possible defensiveness on the part of the receiver, is to ask him or her for an assessment of his or her own performance and the aspects of it he or she believes may need to be worked on. Put into this position people are often inclined to judge themselves more harshly than others would. You are then able to match your assessment of performance against the other person's own assessment. You can balance those points where he or she has been overcritical with a more positive and encouraging appraisal while also working constructively on the aspects you believe the person needs to change.

if you are offering feedback

Feedback that you volunteer unasked may be met with defensiveness. What you mean to be constructive and helpful may be perceived as unjust criticism or unwelcome intrusion. Be aware of this possibility, but don't seek to deal with it by engaging in elaborate preliminaries that may dilute or even negate the message you want to get across. Consider your timing, and try to catch the other person when he or she will be most receptive to what you have to say.

10 pointers for effective feedback

1. *Don't apologise.* By all means acknowledge that you have something to say that may not be entirely comfortable, but profuse apologies give the message that a) you have no right to say what you are saying, and b) what you are saying may not be valid.
2. *Get to the point quickly.* Lengthy introductions may cause your listener to turn off before you arrive at what it is you really want to say.
3. *Don't go over the top with praise.* If you have something critical to say, opening your remarks with some comments about the person's strengths can help to defuse a defensive response, but laying it on too thickly will smack of insincerity.

4. *Check the other person's understanding of what you have said.* Any defensiveness on the part of the other person will increase the chance of misperceptions.

5. *Be proximate.* Feedback is best delivered as soon after the event as possible. If the message is a critical one, then waiting until the next review meeting comes around smacks of harbouring bad feeling. If the feedback is positive then it will have a far more potent effect on performance if it occurs immediately following the behaviour.

6. *Be specific.* Often as givers of feedback we hide behind vague comments that are difficult to challenge but also impossible to unpack. These are not helpful at all. The receiver needs to know precisely what it is about his or her performance that is not working well so as to be able to do something about it.

7. *Own what you say.* Don't hide behind organisational policy or the reported opinions of senior people.

8. *Deal with what is achievable.* For all of us there are limits to how far and how fast we are able to change. A shy and tongue-tied interviewee is not going to be transformed into an ultra-competent performer at one leap. So give people things they can get hold of – incremental steps that will take them along the road to the ultimate goal. It's an extension of the technique we looked at in Chapter 1 in relation to your own goals. Don't load them down with too many points either. It will be disheartening for them and will probably mean that none of the recommendations get tackled properly. Recognise also that there may come a stage for everybody where personality or ability will permit no further change.

9. *Tell the person what you see, not what he or she thinks.* Feedback is your honest impression, which

the receiver may decide to accept or reject. It should not be an attempt by you to get inside the other person's head and tell that person why he or she acted in a particular way. Recognise this in your speech. For example, rather than saying 'Your heart wasn't in this task', say 'It appeared to me as if your heart wasn't in this task.'

10. *Deal with behaviour, not people.* If you are giving feedback that may be interpreted as critical, be sure that you are focusing on the behaviour and not the person. Avoid labelling people with expressions such as 'You're lazy' and don't introduce comparisons – 'If only you could be a bit more like Jenny.'

seeking feedback

We all have an image of ourselves that differs from the way others see us and we may go for years without hearing what people genuinely think about us. Even at an appraisal, perceptions are often dressed up politely to avoid giving offence. So at first sight, seeking feedback from others may appear to risk denting confidence, but in the long term a realistic appreciation of your image in the eyes of others enables you to correct misinterpretations and relieve yourself of the tension and uncertainty that occur whenever you are unsure how you are coming across.

how to seek feedback

1. Pick the right person. He or she needs to be someone you trust and are able to be relaxed with. Obviously you will want to feel that this person is not the type to use the opportunity to score over you. But neither do you want to approach a sycophant who will only tell

you what he or she thinks you want to hear. Go for somebody who you know deals in truth. If you approach the wrong person, you'll get the wrong answer.

2. Let the person know that you are asking him or her because you value his or her opinion. Emphasise that what you are looking for is balanced, constructive criticism – that you want to know what you have done right as well as what you may have done wrong.

3. Don't just ask the person out of the blue what he or she thinks of you. Most people faced with this sort of request will be startled and embarrassed, and will give you watered-down versions of their real opinions. Give thought beforehand to the things you want to know about, and give some leads. 'I'm concerned that I might be coming over as rather distant with people in the office. Is it true?'

4. Seek specific examples of the things you have done well and not so well. Ask for practical suggestions on what you might do differently in future.

5. Having raised the points you want to hear about, listen to the responses. Don't get defensive about things that may be uncomfortable. They could be misperceptions on the part of the person you are talking to, but provided you have set up the exchange properly, they will be genuinely held ones.

6. Remember to thank the person for the feedback even if it has been uncomfortable.

accepting praise and recognition

All that I have written about setting one's own criteria for success is not intended to diminish the value of praise and recognition. They should be welcome and confidence-building.

It is simply over-reliance on receiving praise that you should avoid. Paradoxically, however, many people whose self-esteem is not high have great difficulty accepting recognition. They may be embarrassed, suspicious or dismissive – resorting to excessive modesty with some mumbled self-deprecating remarks that lessen the chance of further recognition coming from the same source. The person offering the praise receives the impression that it is being thrown back. If any of this strikes a chord with you, give some thought to how you will deal with praise in future. Accepting it is as much of a skill as giving it. A little modesty is fine, but recognise that when you have done a good job you have a right to accept the plaudits. Do so with grace and more will come your way.

bullying

Bullying has always existed in the workplace and has always been immensely damaging to the confidence and effectiveness of targeted individuals, but recent research indicates that the problem is becoming more widespread. And it is not a phenomenon whose victims are solely to be found among junior staff. A survey carried out by the UK Institute of Personnel and Development found that professional and managerial staff are just as likely to be targeted.

The archetypal workplace bully is somebody who picks on those he or she perceives to be weaker and submits them to a climate of unpredictability and fear through tantrums, intimidating behaviour, threats and humiliation. But not all bullies operate in this conveniently visible way. They may also:

- constantly find fault, nit-pick and criticise;
- undermine the targeted individual – spreading rumours, removing responsibilities without good cause, ostracising, allocating menial jobs;
- unfairly manipulate workload and resources – set impossible deadlines, make unreasonable demands, withhold necessary resources.

Workplace bullies tend to be higher in the pecking order than their victims, but this is by no means always the case. Bullying occurs between people at the same level and there are even cases of people bullying their superiors. In some professions such as education and the health service, staff may be on the receiving end of bullying clients. The classic bully is a person who has low self-esteem and uses the behaviour as an attempt to bolster his or her security and status at the expense of others.

There may be a second category of bully who is responding to circumstances rather than behaving in consequence of psychological problems. In an increasingly pressurised working environment such people are reacting to the demands they themselves are facing. They are stressed as a result of overload with which they can't cope and are passing the pressure down the line. Their bullying behaviour may be about unleashing some of the anger they feel in relation to the pressure they find themselves under or may arise from sheer desperation to get things done. Cary Cooper, professor of organisational psychology at the University of Manchester Institute of Science and Technology, maintains that while the numbers of classic bullies remain fairly constant, there are increasing numbers of those whose behaviour is a response to overload.

There is no simple answer to dealing with a bully, but one thing is certain – if you do nothing, you can look forward to continuation of the trouble with all the attendant misery and damage to your self-belief. If you have worked in a team or department with a bullying boss, you will have noticed that some people get victimised much more frequently than others – some not at all. Those who suffer most are the ones perceived by the bully to have some area of vulnerability – perhaps they lack assertiveness, are particularly self-deprecating, have a need to feel valued. Or perhaps it is that they are different in some way to other members of the team – different tastes and views, a tendency to be more isolated.

I'm not suggesting that you seek to change your views and personality to combat bullying, but some of the confidence-enhancing strategies covered elsewhere in this book will help to prevent you becoming a victim:

▓ Work on being more assertive in your day-to-day dealings.

▓ Make yourself less dependent on the approval of others.

▓ Seek some alliances with like-minded individuals.

▓ Don't let your body language or speech send out submissive signals. Draw yourself up to your full height, don't stoop, maintain eye contact and eliminate any self-disparaging messages from what you say. Expressions like 'Oh, my views don't count for anything' almost invite people to victimise you.

facing up to the bully

From where I sit, I cannot judge the nature of your workplace or the scale of your boss's psychosis, so it would be irresponsible for me to make a sweeping statement such as 'The only way to deal with a bully is to face up to him or her.' But sooner or later somebody has to, and if you are able to do it, you may be able to free yourself at a stroke and raise your own self-belief in the process. There is a risk involved, but it's another of those occasions to ask yourself 'What is the worst possible outcome?' and weigh the possible risk against the benefits.

Assuming you decide to raise the issue with the bully, it's important not to get emotional or fly off the handle. If you lose control, then the bully has achieved the power over you that he or she is seeking. So the name of the game is: calm, controlled and assertive.

▓ Be clear in your mind beforehand what behaviour you are unhappy about.

■ Tell the person coherently and unequivocally what he or she has done that you believe to be unreasonable and unfair.

■ Be specific. If you are complaining immediately following the behaviour this is straightforward, but if your complaint relates to a pattern of behaviour over time then it helps to have a record of specific instances. Don't let the bully trivialise the complaint by homing in on just one incident.

■ Be prepared for attempts to belittle your complaint or to throw it back on to you – 'You're just being silly and emotional' or 'If you can't stand the heat, get out of the kitchen.' Stand your ground. It is not your fault; it is the bully's problem and he or she must be made aware of it.

Even if you get through to the bully, don't expect instant results. You may need to return to the issue on several occasions before you see a change in attitude. But once you have summoned the courage on the first occasion, subsequent encounters tend to be less difficult. Stick to the same formula – calm and firm. Your bully is unlikely to acknowledge his or her behaviour, but don't confuse reaction with outcome. The reaction to your complaint may be disgruntled, offhand, puzzled or offensive, but if you notice some ensuing change then you've had an effect. Celebrate any changes, and if you feel the person is really making an effort to treat you with greater respect, give some positive feedback. Even bullies respond to praise.

It is possible that the person is not aware of his or her bullying behaviour. Because the behaviour arises from a sense of personal inadequacy, there is a tendency towards self-deception – bullies seeing their behaviour simply as tough management. But it is not always just denial. As a personnel director dealing with instances of bullying, I recall occasions when bullies appeared genuinely shocked that their behaviour should have caused offence. This was particularly prevalent when the bullying behaviour seemed to have arisen out of pressure that the manager was under.

seeking assistance

There is no reason to regard the involvement of others as an indication of weakness on your part. Seeking some assistance is a sensible and proactive thing to do, and far preferable to enduring the behaviour. Simply putting up with bullying may damage more than your confidence at work. The stress it causes can affect your work performance, your health and your home life.

colleagues

A sensible first step may be to sound out trusted colleagues to see whether anyone else is being similarly affected by the same person's behaviour. If so, there could be mutual support or a possible joint approach to the individual or management. Failing this, there is still considerable value to be had from talking the situation through with a friend or colleague. In addition to a welcome friendly ear and moral support, your colleague may be able to help you to articulate your complaint and assist you in dealing with it more assertively. He or she might also have a contribution to make in identifying any behaviours on your part that make you more susceptible to bullying. If you are a member of a union or professional association then it may be worth while discussing your complaint with them. Bullying is an issue on which all the major unions have clear policies and guidelines, and is generally regarded as a high priority issue for them.

management

An approach to management inevitably raises the level of formality, but do not be deterred by the thought that you will be considered weak and silly. There is a growing awareness of bullying and many larger companies and public organisations now have anti-bullying policies. If the person you are complaining about is your own manager, then you will need to go to the next level up, or to the personnel department if there is one. You will need to decide whether you wish to make the approach alone or be accompanied by a friend or representative. Don't present your complaint in an apologetic manner. Remember that it is your right not to be treated in a bullying fashion. Victims of bullying who are themselves in management positions are often the most reluctant to take up a complaint formally, feeling that it is an admission of inadequacy on their part. Dismiss this notion: managers get bullied too.

Once you have taken the decision to involve a third party it is most important that you marshal your facts. Bullies often have a Jekyll and Hyde tendency – vicious in private, charming and reasonable in public – and can be consummate liars. If you find yourself reaching a formal grievance stage it could be your word against the bully's. It's important, well before it comes to that, to have specific evidence:

- Keep records of incidents to which you can refer, including dates and times.
- Keep copies of any correspondence that may support your case.
- It is a good idea to document incidents that might otherwise become just anecdotal evidence. For example, if your boss has attempted to saddle you with impossible demands, send him or her a memo detailing the reasons you believe them to be unreasonable.

external advice

If your own efforts are not bearing fruit or you need advice before proceeding to more formal stages, there are a number of organisations and Web sites dedicated to providing such assistance. A good example is the UK National Bullying Advice Line (tel: 01235 212286; Web site: www.successunlimited.co.uk). It combines excellent advice with an online support forum and details of local support groups. The Advisory Conciliation and Arbitration Service (ACAS) offers advice leaflets aimed at both employees and employers. If your health is suffering, a visit to your GP may be called for. The ultimate sanction might be to resign and claim constructive dismissal in an industrial tribunal, but this is a course that should only be contemplated as a last resort and with the benefit of expert advice.

coping with crises

Which of the following constitutes a crisis?

- A key member of your team is rushed into hospital after a suspected heart attack.
- The payroll program crashes on the day you are due to transmit salary information for bank payment.
- A supplier phones to say that essential materials due for delivery tomorrow will not be available for another four weeks.
- A newspaper advertisement you have placed contains incorrect telephone contact numbers.

The answer, of course, is that they all may be. But whether events constitute crises depends largely on our perception of them. We have all met people for whom the slightest departure from the norm is a reason to press the panic button, and also those who appear unmoved by even the most cataclysmic of events. Our own reactions to events vary according to the other pressures we are facing. I recall noticing, some years ago, that my crises seemed particularly prevalent on Friday afternoons. There wasn't anything sinister about that end of the week. It was just that in a stressful job and working long hours, I had lost some of my resilience by the time Friday came around.

With that came a tendency to intensify events that might not have been perceived as quite so critical in the earlier part of the week. So the first lesson about crises lies in when and if you choose to define them as such. Whenever you feel you are facing a crisis, ask yourself whether there is anything that may be distorting your perception of the situation. Going into crisis mode unnecessarily will not benefit you in any way.

A crisis is a situation which:

- occurs suddenly and unexpectedly;
- suggests the need for a swift response;
- is likely to lead to further problems if not dealt with;
- may threaten loss and embarrassment for the individual or the organisation.

Quite clearly the term can be used to describe a huge range of conditions, from the minor personal problem to the full-blown organisational emergency. Given the personal focus of this book, I shall confine myself to consideration of the minor to moderate end of the scale. The principles of dealing with major crises are not too different, but start to raise such issues as crisis planning, crisis management teams and media communication, none of which we have space for. There are a number of books on crisis management for any reader who wishes to investigate the subject more deeply.

So how does a crisis damage your confidence? Well, for starters it tends to take over, consigning your plans and priorities to the bin. It may threaten your reputation and leave you feeling stressed, indecisive and out of control. On the other hand, the experience of weathering crises successfully can provide a significant confidence boost.

how not to react

■ **Rabbit in the headlights**
Faced with the oncoming danger, the requirement for swift action and the possible consequences of choosing the wrong option, rabbits are transfixed by indecision and flattened in the road.

■ **Bull**
Unlike the rabbits, bulls are galvanised into immediate action. Their weakness is a tendency to charge at the first solution to enter their field of vision without adequate consideration of alternative courses of action.

■ **Hedgehog**
Hedgehogs don't suffer the rabbit's indecision. They have a tried and tested means of dealing with impending danger. It may serve them quite well if the threat is a small one. Unfortunately it doesn't work too well with 40-tonne lorries.

These three typical responses – indecision, impetuosity and avoidance – are understandable if unwise. At the very time we most need careful consideration of the situation and calm decision making, they desert us. So, if you're not going to be a rabbit, a bull or a hedgehog, how should you deal with crises? Well, not surprisingly, it's a matter once again of putting yourself in control as far as you can. The rest of this chapter concentrates on how you might do that.

reducing the likelihood of crises

Tight deadlines and overly ambitious targets put you at risk of setbacks becoming crises. Nothing will ever go quite as smoothly as you hope, so if it's possible to do so, build some flexibility into your plans and schedules. Without introducing unnecessary fears into your work, give some thought to things that could go wrong. Keep an eye open for the people who are liable to cause crises – loose cannons and those who are inclined to act without thinking. Monitor closely any activity where there could be a risk of problems getting out of hand. Learn from experience. It's surprising how often similar situations recur. If you are experiencing repeated similar crises, you need to spend some time analysing the reasons for them and how they might be prevented. Make sure that your communication lines are open and effective. Poor communication may trigger a crisis, make it more difficult for you to see it coming and affect your ability to manage it when it occurs.

resisting panic

Panic is a perfectly natural reaction to impending danger. It's the fight or flight response again, only at a more intense level than that we might experience when facing criticism. Just as before, we need a calm response:

- ▓ *Catch it as early as possible.* Panic feeds upon itself and can escalate very quickly. The earlier you act, the easier it is to control.
- ▓ *Use conscious physical activity to control it.* Use deep breathing as described in Chapter 6 to control the physical symptoms of panic and help bring order and balance to your thinking.
- ▓ *Get the situation in proportion.* When you're facing a crisis, it can assume a wholly excessive level of importance. Counteract this tendency to exaggerate the scale of the problem by asking yourself what is the worst that can happen. Seldom is it a matter of life and death. Even the fear that you may be sacked will usually be an overstatement.

▓ *Step outside the situation.* Viewing the crisis objectively helps you to maintain your calm and to explore possible solutions. Discussing the issue with another person who is not connected with it may help you to do this, or you may benefit from taking yourself away from the immediate problem environment for a brief while – a walk around the block, for example. This is not to be confused with avoidance. The breathing space is a necessary part of getting your thoughts straight.

clarifying the main issue

If you fail to do this, you may go haring off in pursuit of unnecessary solutions. Take the case of the payroll computer crash I used as an example earlier. The problem is that employees' salaries are unlikely to be paid into their bank accounts on the normal day and that this will lead to possible serious consequences for them if they have timed commitments such as mortgage payments. Setting up an emergency payment arrangement for the people so affected will probably take precedence over striving to resolve the computer bug and recover the data – especially so if the deadline for bank transfer is going to be missed regardless of how quickly the fault can be resolved.

Ask yourself:

  ▓ What is the precise nature of the problem?
  ▓ Who is it likely to affect?
  ▓ What information do I need in order to clarify the options available to me?
  ▓ What will happen if I do nothing?
  ▓ Whom do I need to involve or consult?
  ▓ What is the timescale for action?
  ▓ What resources are available to me?

---

considering options and deciding strategy

Whatever the circumstances, you need to consider the options available to you. With the pressure on, it's tempting to rush, bull-like, straight from problem to action. Resist it. Considering your options does not have to be a lengthy process, and speed of response is seldom so vital that it outweighs the benefits of a little thought. In some circumstances doing nothing may be a valid option, provided you can satisfy yourself that it is not a choice reached by indecisiveness or avoidance. Depending on the nature of the crisis your strategy may consist of one or more of the following:

- ■ tackling the underlying problem;
- ■ limiting damage caused by the problem;
- ■ communicating the problem and your actions.

The task doesn't finish when you have mapped out your strategy. Crises are often dynamic events and you need to monitor outcomes carefully and, if necessary, adjust your strategy to take account of a changing situation.

communicating

Often, crises are escalated by poor consultation and communication. The person responsible hopes to be able to get the situation under control without anyone becoming aware that something is amiss. But it rapidly becomes apparent to others that all is not well, and in the absence of timely information suspicion and rumour make a bad situation worse.

Consulting your boss should not be a matter of just covering your back or attempting to offload responsibility. You are likely to receive the most favourable response if you consult early and show that not only have you accepted responsibility for dealing with the crisis, but you have already given thought to a plan of action.

Your approach to consultation with others will depend in part on the culture of the organisation you work in, and your relationship with your team. But the most important determinant should be the nature of the problem and the actions to be taken. Think about the degree of consultation appropriate to the circumstances. At one extreme it may simply be a matter of informing people what has happened and what you are doing about it. Where you need the commitment of others in the implementation of solutions, a greater degree of involvement in the decision-making process will be appropriate.

There can't be a crisis next week. My schedule is already full.

Henry Kissinger

tuning in to office politics

Mention the words 'office politics' and people tend to think of some of the more distasteful and confidence-sapping elements of working life: favouritism; intrigue; rumour; backbiting; hidden agendas; individuals advancing their careers at the expense of others. But politics are an inevitable and indeed necessary aspect of any organisation, no matter how well managed. Whatever the field of endeavour, there will always be differences of opinion on the best way to achieve organisational objectives, competition for limited resources and disagreement about the priority to be attached to different aspects of the organisation's work. How these are resolved is down to politics – the business of influencing and persuading. Those who are politically unaware, unskilled or not prepared to play are probably not doing the best for themselves, their teams or even the organisations they work for. Lack of political savvy will prevent you from achieving your goals, leave you adrift from the action and will thereby impact on your confidence. The negative and destructive features of politics will never be entirely absent, although they may be significantly diminished in healthy organisations, but it is possible to be a

political animal without sacrificing honesty and profession-
alism.

Political skill involves the following:

- identifying and accessing key people in the organisation;
- recognising sources of influence and being able to
  maximise one's own influence;
- being able to present one's ideas and proposals persua-
  sively;
- understanding how lobbying may be of benefit;
- maintaining effective and mutually advantageous links
  within and beyond the organisation.

Let's take a look at each of these.

identifying key people

Take a look at the organisation you work in, or at least your
part of it. Who are the key people? They are not necessarily the
ones who sit at the top of the hierarchy. Here are three types
you might think about:

- **Movers**
  There will be some people who have a degree of influence that outstrips their position in the organisation. I
  am not referring here to those whose influence is
  simply down to whom they know, but those who have
  clout that arises from personal qualities, perceived
  expertise, reputation for integrity, skill in communicating, or marketing their abilities. Observe how they
  go about it – there may be things you can learn from
  their success. Such people tend to make useful allies so,
  without turning yourself into a sycophant, see if you

have common ground that will help you work together.

▨ **Gatekeepers**

These are people who have their hands on the flow of information and control over access to others. Again they may not be particularly senior. They may be secretaries or receptionists, for example. Links with them can help you to know what is happening in the organisation, making you less dependent on rumours. Getting to know them may also assist you in gaining the ear of other key individuals.

▨ **Gurus**

These may be seen as the wise elders of the organisation – people who have a mass of acquired experience and knowledge. They can be found at various levels of seniority. Typically they are people whose careers have peaked or who are not desperately pursuing advancement, and therefore do not guard their knowledge as jealously as others who are still trying to make their reputations. They can be invaluable sources of information, advice and feedback.

activity

▨ Who are the people in your organisation that fall into these categories?

▨ Do you have existing links with these people – could you seek information, advice, support on an informal basis if you needed to?

influencing

The amount of influence you have may be down to who you know, who you are, what you know and how well you put yourself across. Leaving aside the first of these for the moment, let's take a look at the others.

position

'I'm the boss, so you'll do it my way.' Using hierarchical position to get things done is strictly more about power than influence. It works because you will generally have control over resources, and be in a position to apply sanctions if you don't get what you want. Some managers never appear to adopt any other approach, seemingly unaware that people who are following a course of action because they have been told to do so are unlikely to be as committed as those who genuinely believe in what they are about. Of course, position power only works in a downwards direction. It has no influence upwards or sideways. People who rely solely on position are often insecure bullies.

expertise

As a source of influence, your expertise is only of any value if the people you may be seeking to influence recognise it and consider it of value. It can be frustrating when they don't, but a gentle, understated reminder to others works a lot better than indignant protestations that your talents are being overlooked.

Which of these statements is more likely to receive a positive response?

> ▨ 'I worked on a project rather like this in my previous job. If you wish, I'd be happy to share some of the things I learnt from it.'

▨ 'I know all about this sort of problem from my previous job. If you would only listen to me, I could tell you how we should be going about it.'

The second statement presents a challenge to other people's skills and knowledge, which may provoke resistance rather than acceptance. And in the event that the speaker's suggestions are taken on board, there is no doubt where fingers will point if anything goes wrong.

If your expertise is regularly overlooked, you might ask yourself why.

Are you:

- ▨ allowing others to take credit for things you have done? ☐
- ▨ keeping too low a profile – not putting yourself about where you will be noticed? ☐
- ▨ overselling your skills and knowledge to the point of putting others off? ☐
- ▨ letting other factors – personality traits, weaknesses, allegiances – prevent others from seeking your views? ☐

Privately, everyone acknowledges that Julie is the most knowledgeable and experienced person in the department. But they avoid seeking her views whenever possible because they regard her as arrogant and resent the way she tries to take over. In truth Julie has not a great deal of self-belief and the behaviour to which her colleagues object is the way she compensates for this. She is unaware how she comes across and her colleagues' failure to draw upon her expertise further damages her confidence.

personal qualities

We cannot all be blessed with the charisma of Martin Luther King. But we do have some sway over personal qualities that play a major part in whether or not we have influence with our colleagues. In large part these are similar qualities to those we looked at in the section on building trust (Chapter 5). You need to be:

- honest and open with people, and able to be counted upon to do what you say;
- ready to share praise and sense of achievement;
- able to see other people's points of view and respond to them;
- willing to take responsibility;
- skilled at listening;
- prepared to trust others.

It's important to demonstrate these qualities in all daily dealings. You have probably met people who turn on the 'trust me' routine when they think it's needed, but the rest of the time behave in a manner that would make Machiavelli blush. It doesn't work.

Don't try to adopt a persona that is unnatural or uncomfortable for you. Just be natural and develop your own style. A person who comes over as forced or less than genuine is liable to be regarded with some suspicion. Finally, try to be positive and proactive. It may not be easy if you are working in a climate characterised by whingeing and negativity, but even in such environments people who are able to maintain their enthusiasm and to pitch themselves into challenges get listened to and get results.

persuading

Persuasiveness is by no means just down to slick language. Indeed, in some circumstances, pressure salesmanship can be a real disadvantage. Nor will logic on its own be sufficient to see you through. While you clearly need the ability to assemble an argument and to spot the flaws in those of others, even the most cogently argued of proposals may founder if it is not accompanied by attention to the attitudes and reactions of those to whom it is addressed, and by recognition of political realities in the organisation:

▓ **Think about what you are proposing**
  - What alternative courses of action are there?
  - Why are they less desirable than the proposal you are making?
  - What will you settle for if you don't get everything you are looking for?
▓ **Get a critical friend to subject your proposal to scrutiny**
  - What different perspectives can your critical friend bring to bear upon it?
  - What things have you not thought about?
  - How may you need to amend the proposal in the light of your critical friend's comments?
▓ **Think about timing**
  This will not always be within your control, but a proposal that in every other respect is excellent may fail because it is poorly timed. Try to avoid times when the people you are hoping to convince will be distracted by other pressing matters. Also, steer clear of hitting people with more than they can handle at any one time. It may be possible to present just an outline or to go for an incremental approach rather than presenting a comprehensive bundle of proposals, which may all be rejected.

- ▒ **Think about the people you are seeking to convince**
  - Who are they? Are they homogeneous or composed of disparate groups?
  - What knowledge can you take for granted? What will you need to spell out? Will this vary for different parts of your audience? Remember that other people will not necessarily share the frame of reference that has allowed you to come to the conclusions you have. The problem may be obvious to you, but need to be spelt out to others.
  - How will you check their understanding?
  - How will you approach them – one-to-one discussion, informal gathering, formal meeting/presentation?
  - How will you tailor what you have to say in order to meet the varied levels of understanding among your audience?

using questions as a persuasion technique

A questioning approach will generally be more productive than a full-frontal hard sell. In dealing with questions, your listener is sharing the process with you, helping to define the problem and identify the solutions. Questions assist you in gathering information, developing rapport, raising awareness, checking understanding and reinforcing the commitment of those you are seeking to persuade.

Information gathering starts from a desire to understand the perspective of others. Do their experiences on the issue line up with your own? Do they have additional information that may modify or reinforce the solutions you have in mind? This sort of questioning also assists in building rapport, in that you are demonstrating readiness to listen to the others' views and possibly to make amendments to your proposals.

Awareness-raising is achieved by asking questions on which you already have a pretty good idea of the likely answers you will get. Through them, you lead those you are seeking to persuade to a greater realisation of the problem and the solutions you are proposing. Take care not to make leaps of understanding that are too large or too quick for your audience. You will have already done a lot of thinking about the issue, but your audience may be coming to it fresh and without your detailed knowledge. You may need to continue asking questions well beyond the point at which you feel the problem has been defined and links to the proposed solution established.

Questioning to check understanding is a vital part of the process. It is all too easy to charge ahead, on the assumption that your audience is with you, when in fact you have left them floundering over a previous point. Take opportunities to draw the threads together and ask questions like 'Does this make sense?', 'Is there anything you think I may have left out?' and 'Are there other examples that you can give?'

Finally, questioning builds commitment. If the people you are seeking to persuade feel that they have been involved in defining the problem and arriving at the solution, they are more likely to be committed to it. It is something that is jointly owned rather than a proposal you are trying to foist upon them.

lobbying

Lobbying is the process of generating support for a point of view in advance of a meeting at which a decision is to be taken. People are more inclined to stick with a view that they take with them into a meeting than they are to be won over by something they hear in the course of it. Your confidence will be boosted if you are able to go there knowing that you can count on the support of a number of those present. But lobbying needs to be done with care. Handled ineptly it may be perceived as undue pressure or even bullying. You are most likely to succeed if you approach people in the spirit of obtaining their views, indicating readiness to make adjustments to your proposal in the light of them. Information-gathering and awareness-raising questions, as outlined above, will probably figure prominently.

networking

Whereas lobbying is about eliciting support for specific proposals, networking is the formation of links and allegiances that may be of use in the future. The term may conjure images of old boy networks – invisible strings pulled between shadowy figures. But while not everything to do with networking is always entirely wholesome, it would be a great mistake to dismiss something that is in the main ethical and can provide a significant boost to your performance, influence and career progression:

▓ **Performance**
Networking can provide you with important information and intelligence relevant to your job, as well as access to the skills and experience of others. When you are facing a tricky problem, the opportunity to talk it through with someone else who has faced a similar issue can be a considerable boost to confidence, and heightens the chance of making the right decision.

▓ **Influence**
You raise your profile through networking. Other people remember you and what you have to offer. You give yourself a greater chance of being consulted on issues that call for your expertise and experience.

▓ **Career progression**
Only a minority of career opportunities are filled through advertisement. The person who networks

effectively has a greater chance of being headhunted. Even in jobs appointed by advertisement, candidates with known track record and visible profile are generally favoured over anonymous applicants.

building a network

Although it is possible to see all your working relationships as one big network, we will concentrate here on the business of building and maintaining relationships with people you would not encounter in your normal day-to-day activity. The process has all the features discussed in the chapter on building relationships but, because your network is composed of those you must seek out rather than people with whom you are thrown together, it requires greater effort on your part to initiate, cultivate and maintain links.

You may have networks across the organisation you work for – people who work in different departments or on different sites – or external contacts in other organisations. Be conscious of the balance between internal and external networks. If your contacts are exclusively internal and the organisation you work for is relatively small, you may be restricting your profile and limiting progression opportunities. If your contacts and focus are mainly external, you may acquire a reputation as somebody who is simply looking to move elsewhere.

Building your network might mean:

▨ remaining in touch with former colleagues who have moved on to pastures new;

▨ making the most of membership of professional associations;

▨ making an effort to talk to new people you meet at meetings, conferences and training events;

▨ participating in social or recreational activities associated with your workplace or occupational group.

Networks aren't put together overnight; they have to develop over a period of time. Some people like to set themselves targets – to cultivate a certain number of new contacts each year. That may sound a bit too calculating, but it does work. It prompts you to overcome your reticence and open up to people you meet at business events rather more than you might otherwise be inclined.

It is the business of breaking the ice that is the most difficult. For those whose confidence is not at its sharpest, the idea of starting up conversations in new situations can be very daunting. Here's a common example.

> It's one of those sessions that seem to precede every conference or training session. You've registered, been given an enormous badge with your name spelt wrongly and are now trying to juggle a cup of coffee and a large folder of conference papers. You look around the room for a familiar face – nobody! Everyone else appears to be in first-name backslapping groups. You sip your coffee and long to be invisible.

Few people are really comfortable in such situations. But the chances are that there will be other newcomers who are feeling just as uncertain as you, and even those seemingly impregnable groups may be nowhere near as cliquey as they appear at first glance. So confront the fear – you are not going to be rejected or ridiculed – and make a move. It's never as hard as you think it's going to be.

You don't have to introduce yourself with something witty or profound. Questions make the best opening gambit. Don't worry about them being routine or boring. People like to talk about themselves, so any question that helps them to do that – where they come from, what sort of job they do – will get the ball rolling.

Breaking into seemingly established groups is always harder

than starting up conversations with individuals. You worry about appearing pushy or finding that once you have muscled into the group you have nothing to contribute. You will find it easier if you are open about your predicament. 'Hi! I seem to be in the position where I don't know anybody here. Do you mind if I join you?'

more tips on networking

Don't be too calculating about it. The most successful networkers are those who are interested in people, enjoy inter-action and are prepared to give something of themselves. The person who only strikes up relationships on the basis of perceived career value will frequently get it wrong, and will acquire a reputation for toadyism to boot.

Recognise that networking relationships are about mutual benefit. If you are approaching somebody you believe may be a useful new contact, think about what value you may be to that person as well as his or her usefulness to you.

Remember that networks do not end with your direct contacts. The people you are in touch with have contacts of their own. A good mutually beneficial relationship is one where either party can pick up the phone and say, 'I'm working on this tricky problem at the moment. Do you know anyone with such and such experience I might be able to approach for advice?'

maintaining networks

Some relationships can stand long periods of silence, whereas others need regular contact if they are to be maintained. Of course, you can't expect to keep up all your contacts indefi-nitely; people will come and go. But have an eye to those with whom it is particularly important to remain in contact. You will know who the significant people are – those who have been there with help and advice on the most troubling problems. But as your life and career develop it's all too easy to lose touch, so make a special effort with the people you value most. I'm sure you don't need me to spell out ways of keeping in touch. Just be sure it doesn't become wholly ritualised.

working in a negative climate

You may be unlucky enough to find yourself working in a negative climate – perhaps in a team whose primary character- istics are moaning and destructiveness, or, worse, in a situation where the entire organisation is riddled with negativity. In either case you can see your enthusiasm and confidence disap- pearing down the plughole. Within a team the tone is generally set by one or two dominant individuals, and social acceptance in some offices is dependent on subscribing to the majority line. Organisation-wide negativity is generally a feature of poor management or rapid change. It is manifest in:

- ▓ poor official communication and an overactive grape- vine;
- ▓ lack of clear direction;
- ▓ suspicion of management motives;
- ▓ frequent shifts in policy;
- ▓ high staff turnover and absenteeism;
- ▓ a blame culture;
- ▓ rival factions and turf wars among managers;
- ▓ hazy or erratic management of performance.

In some occupations that have undergone major changes in recent years, the negative atmosphere may extend beyond the organisation to embrace a whole sector of employment. For example, some recent studies in the UK have pointed to conspicuously low levels of job satisfaction and high incidence of disillusionment in the teaching profession and parts of the civil service.

So, what do you do if you are in a negative environment? Well, the options are three: put up with it, seek to change it or get out. Putting up with it may seem the easiest thing to do. You can build yourself a shell, limit your interaction and get on with your job. But long term this can be very wearing. If it is possible to take more active steps then this is what I would advise.

Avoid the Jeremiahs. The worst offenders tend to be people who aren't too good at their jobs and have little interest in helping others, although they often talk a good line about the support they provide for colleagues. This 'support' consists of encouragement to wallow in their own brand of negativity and, of course, offers further excuses to whinge about the deficiencies of management.

Seek out instead those committed to positive thinking, humour or survival. In even the most negative teams or organisations they do exist. They are unlikely to publicise their presence as markedly as the whingers, so it's a case of keeping your eyes and ears open and developing your networking skills.

Don't assume that a predominantly negative team climate enjoys the support of everyone in it. There will be those who are going for an easy life, keeping their heads down, but who could be turned around to a more positive way of thinking and behaving. If you are able to take a proactive role and with the help of one or two others inject a more positive tone, you may find that you start to carry the silent majority with you.

If you are in a management or supervisory position, isolate those things that you are able to do something about and work upon them. For example, you may not be in a position to do much about overall organisational direction or factors that may be the result of external forces – changes in government policy or funding uncertainty. But you can, perhaps, compensate for this within the area of your responsibility by giving as much attention as possible to ensuring clear, reasonable and consistent expectations, timely and effective communication and a consultative style of management. Use positive feedback immediately to reward instances of contribution to team goals and positive climate.

If, despite every effort, you cannot detect any change, and the negativity continues to get you down, then the answer may be to move on. In such circumstances you will need to weigh the advantages and disadvantages. Plus points may include the opportunity to start afresh, to renew your confidence and possibly to advance your career. Minus points might be the need to retrain or move into a different area of work. Often it is fear of the unknown that keeps people plugging away in a negative environment for far longer than is good for them.

combating stress

Stress is widely accepted as being endemic in the modern work-place, and we are regularly reminded of its physical and psychological consequences. Numerous authoritative studies have pointed to the inexorable rise in anxiety, depression and burnout among workers throughout the developed world. There is not the space in this book to permit a serious study of all aspects of work-related stress, but as it is both a cause and a consequence of reduced confidence, it is important that we give it some attention.

We associate stress with:

- excessive workloads;
- tight deadlines;
- uncertainty and change;
- events that we are unable to control;
- harassment and bullying.

But we should also remind ourselves that stress is not something to be avoided at all costs. We all need a certain level of stress in order to perform well. The positive side of stress is about raising our game to meet challenges, and that increase in performance has a clear feedback in terms of enhanced self-belief. There comes a stage, however, when additional pressure

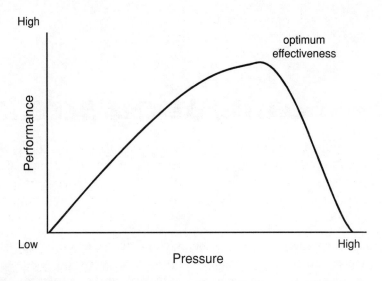

Figure 10.1 *Performance curve*

has a negative effect on performance. Figure 10.1 illustrates the relationship between pressure and performance.

When there is very little pressure upon us we are likely to experience boredom and frustration. Our abilities are under-utilised and confidence can suffer as a result. Increased pressure offers a greater degree of challenge and stimulation to perform, and we behave more creatively, decisively and effectively. There comes a point at the top of the curve where pressure is at the level to produce optimum performance. Beyond that point any further pressure drags us down – we suffer from overload, indecision, anxiety, procrastination and loss of confidence. Whether or not we stay in the positive range or tip over into negative stress is determined by various factors. They include:

▓ awareness of pressure signals;
▓ perceptions of and attitudes towards the threat or challenge;

- self-imposed stress;
- the demands on our time and energy;
- our coping skills.

awareness of the signs

It would be wonderful if we were able to gauge exactly the amount of stress needed to keep ourselves at or near peak performance and to ensure that we never exceeded that quantity. We can't – there are just too many factors impacting upon us and they have a cumulative effect. The various pressures associated with work may be overlaid with home worries, relationship difficulties, financial problems, or health concerns. Alongside the stresses that other people impose are those pressures we have created ourselves in striving to meet our goals. In the modern work environment we are always pushing to get the best out of ourselves and are in danger of going past the point where the negative effects kick in. We need to be conscious of the signals of stress.

Here are some of the more common signs. You will appreciate, of course, that the relationship between stress and the body is a complex one, and that while any of these physical symptoms may indicate stress, they could also arise from other causes. If any of them are serious or prolonged you should consider a visit to your doctor:

- muscle tension – particularly neck pain, hunched shoulders, jaw clenching;
- headaches;
- indigestion;
- nervous twitches;
- changed sleep patterns – difficulty getting to sleep, early waking;
- bowel disturbance;

■ loss of sexual interest;
■ changed eating and drinking habits;
■ lethargy;
■ frequent minor illnesses;
■ increased anxiety;
■ difficulty in determining priorities;
■ irritability and impatience;
■ indecisiveness;
■ problems concentrating and remembering;
■ tendency to make silly mistakes;
■ flitting from task to task, never completing anything;
■ tearfulness;
■ feeling overwhelmed and unable to cope.

It's important to listen to your body and to be alive to any changes in your moods or behaviour. The sooner you act to defuse stress, the better. But the effects can be insidious and it's not always easy to spot them until you are well down the road. What's more, it may be difficult to spot what precisely is causing the stress. You might like to consider recording in your diary feelings and irritations on the day they occur. This can assist you in recognising patterns and pinpointing causes, so that you are better able to determine future strategies. But the diary should not just be a vehicle for diagnosing ills. As mentioned in Chapter 2, it is also a place to engage in positive self-talk and to record achievements made and challenges overcome.

I made the point earlier that pressure may have a positive impact on performance, but there are some forms of pressure that will only ever be negative. So while a work deadline may stimulate you to lift your performance, it's hard to see how the pressure of commuting daily into a busy city on crowded public transport or gridlocked vehicles can be anything other than a negative factor. Identifying and seeking to reduce the wholly negative forms of pressure is one way of reducing the cumulative impact of stress.

perceptions of stress

Confidence is closely linked to our perceptions of how well we are coping with the situations that make up our daily lives. On the rising part of the curve in Figure 10.1, we are on top of things – competently handling whatever is thrown at us – and confidence is boosted. On the falling part, however, we are beset by a perception of failure to cope and our confidence declines. That decline in confidence can itself feed further stress. Problems we might consider trivial at other times are exaggerated and we can fall into a spiral of decline.

While the most extreme of stressors will be quite unambiguous, there is a large grey area in which it is down to you whether you perceive an occurrence as a threat to your well-being or a challenge to overcome. This difference of perception will vary, not only from person to person, but for the same person at different times. Resilient people are generally those who can look for the most positive aspects in any situation. So use the same strategy as we discussed in Chapter 2 on overcoming setbacks. Ask yourself questions such as 'What can I learn from this?' and 'How will this experience help me to be stronger in the future?'

self-imposed stress

How many of the following apply to you?

	Occasionally	Usually	Always
I am easily irritated about small things.	☐	☐	☐
I set myself over-ambitious goals.	☐	☐	☐

	Occasionally	Usually	Always
I don't allow enough time for tasks.	☐	☐	☐
I am late for appointments.	☐	☐	☐
I am highly competitive.	☐	☐	☐
I get very impatient whenever I have to wait in a queue.	☐	☐	☐
I try to do several things at once.	☐	☐	☐

If you have answered usually or always to any of these, then there is a likelihood that you are needlessly presenting yourself with excessive stress. Three or more such responses and you are probably someone who displays what has been termed Type A behaviour.

The concept of Type A and Type B behaviour emanates from the work, some 40 years ago, of two US cardiologists, Friedman and Rosenman. Type A people are characterised as impatient, over-ambitious, over-competitive, irritable and with a constant sense of time urgency. Type B people, on the other hand, are more calm, controlled and easygoing. While they may still be ambitious individuals, they tend not to push themselves as hard and are more capable of handling pressure. Over the years much has been made of the association between Type A behaviour and an increased likelihood of heart disease. Research suggests that while there may be some genetic aspects to Type A characteristics they are, in the main, learnt behaviour and as such are capable of change. Unfortunately, the culture in many modern workplaces actively encourages this type of behaviour even though it may not be hugely effective.

modifying behaviour

Consider those occasions when you succumb to anger, impatience etc. How often is it a help and how often a hindrance in achieving the results you are seeking? Be honest. Isn't it true that for the most part your impatience only results in a hike in stress levels and does nothing to get the job done any better or any quicker? I'm not trying to preach here. I freely admit to having more than my fair share of Type A characteristics and I have been guilty of every ridiculous over-the-top response you can imagine. My long-suffering computer monitor will bear witness to the number of times I have thumped it in frustration at glitches when even a technophobic monkey could have worked out that only calm and methodical action would succeed in locating and resolving whatever the problem might be. So admission out of the way, if you can accept it from a self-confessed sinner, here is a strategy for change.

A general resolution to resist the tendency to become angry and impatient is hard to stick to. So make a start by concentrating on a few of the situations that occur most frequently. Particularly fruitful are those where anger and impatience bring no result whatsoever – waiting at traffic lights, for example. Work on controlling impatience in this limited number of situations for a couple of weeks. Find the humour in your normal behaviour – laughter diffuses anger – and use your success as a springboard to tackle more challenging situations. Reward yourself whenever you are able to keep your cool in circumstances that would normally make you angry. When you feel the anger rising up, use mental self-talk to diffuse it. Ask yourself what it will achieve, and repeat to yourself a simple affirmation such as 'calm approach, better results'.

getting off your own back

If you are inclined to generate your own pressure, by setting yourself overly ambitious targets, trying to do too much in a limited time or striving for perfection, ease up and be a little kinder to yourself. I am not advocating that you settle for inadequate standards, just that you take on board the notion that perfection is seldom possible. Even when it is, the additional effort and stress involved in getting from excellent to the pinnacle of perfection may far outweigh the benefits. Remember also that you don't have to put the same effort and commitment into everything. For some tasks, good or even average is quite sufficient. There is no suggestion here, either, that you let up on your goals. As we have already seen, it is possible to have goals that are well out of reach, but to make progress towards them in small, measured, achievable steps, and to recognise that it is sometimes necessary to take steps sideways or even backwards without losing sight of your objective.

One of the biggest mistakes you can make when under negative pressure is to keep plugging away in the hope that it will eventually come right. Adding extra pressure when you are on the downward side of the curve will only hasten the descent. You need to ease the pressure in some way if you are to regain your equilibrium.

demands on our time

When you are bouncing off the walls of your office it seems impossible to imagine that there is anything you can do to reduce the demands upon you and thereby the stress you are under. But there always is. We will look at a number of them in the next chapter – *keeping on top of your workload*. But remember that pressure comes from many different angles. Each individual source may be perfectly manageable, but when piled on top of one another problems arise. The source of the stress doesn't matter – work, home, leisure – the cumulative effect is the same. So take care to balance the pressures in the various areas of your life, and ensure that you are not having to deal with too many issues at once. Even if they are desirable activities, they can add to the stress.

coping strategies

Some of the coping skills required for dealing with stress are covered in other parts of this book. They include: facing up to fears; bouncing back from setbacks; learning to say no when necessary; combating procrastination. These are all about mental resilience but, as we have already seen, there is a physical dimension to stress, and we can make significant advances in our ability to cope with it through physical exercise and relaxation.

exercise and fitness

Our reactions to pressure are rooted back in the mists of our evolution. We respond to perceived threat by putting the body on red alert – it's our old friend the flight or fight response again. This gearing up of our bodies to provide a physical response, which then does not occur, lies behind many stress-related illnesses. Exercise provides an outlet that is otherwise unavailable in our modern sedentary lifestyle – allowing us harmlessly to return our bodies to a state of equilibrium in the manner that was originally intended.

In addition to the stress-reducing benefits of exercise, there are other confidence-building consequences that should not be ignored. Improved body image and the satisfaction of achieving physical targets can provide a confidence boost that spills over into other areas of activity. And by lifting your overall physical capacity, exercise allows you to cruise through your day at what was previously your flat-out speed.

However, in an increasingly pressured work environment there is evidence that, far from taking more exercise, people are taking less. A 1999 study of working adults carried out by the British Heart Foundation confirms a national trend towards a more intensive working day with fewer breaks and longer hours. Over half of those surveyed believed that the amount of time spent working limited their ability to exercise.

So, when you don't have time for all the things you are currently supposed to be doing, and the pressure on your working day doesn't look like declining, how do you manage to fit in some physical activity? Well, 20 to 30 minutes three or four times a week are all you need. Here are six ways to make sure you get it:

1. *Mobilise the power of habit.* There are things you do every day and barely think about. If you make exercise one of these – as much a part of your daily routine as cleaning your teeth – you will cut down on planning and preparation time. Irregular exercisers are constantly having to remotivate themselves to start up again. Make exercise a priority in your day, not something that can be dropped whenever things gets tight. Scheduling it at regular times will help, but don't become too rigid or obsessive.

2. *Change your attitude towards exercise.* If the thought of exercise fills you with dread, it's going to use up more of your time than necessary. We are all inclined to waste time putting off things we don't want to do. Remove this tendency by changing the way you view exercise. Vary your activities to maintain interest. Focus on the sense of well-being rather than the discomfort. Introduce a social element into exercise for greater enjoyment, and don't use exercise as a form of punishment session to remove guilt about overindulging.

3. *Snatch exercise opportunities at work.* Opportunities for sustained aerobic activity at work are limited, but other forms of beneficial exercise, such as stretching, can be done anywhere and at any time. Stretching reduces stress and fatigue, fosters mental alertness, improves circulation and flexibility, and prepares the body for other physical activity. There are several inexpensive books offering safe stretching routines, some

of which are particularly aimed at office workers and can be carried out at your desk. An example is *Stretching at Your Computer or Desk* by Bob and Jean Anderson (1997, Shelter Publications, Bolinas, CA). Utilising the exercise potential of everyday activities can also pay dividends. Use stairs rather than lifts wherever possible, and whenever your work takes you to another building, walk briskly rather than strolling. This may not seem like the foundation of super-fitness, but every little helps.

4. *Make use of your journey to or from work.* If you live within a reasonable distance of your workplace, then walking, cycling or running may offer significant daily exercise during time when you would otherwise be sitting in traffic. The biggest difficulty is what to do with your clothes and any paperwork or equipment you normally transport between home and work. A specialist running rucksack or cycle panniers may be the answer, or perhaps you can make an arrangement with a colleague who lives nearby and is prepared to transport clothing and equipment for you. If you travel to work by public transport, consider getting off at an earlier stop and walking the remaining distance.

5. *Use natural breaks in your day.* Fitting your exercise into natural breaks helps you to approach the next stage in your day with renewed vigour. For too many of us, lunch consists of a sandwich snatched at our desks. If this applies to you, perhaps you could think about taking a proper break and combining it with some exercise – a brisk walk, jog, swim or gym session if facilities are available. Take the exercise before you eat and be realistic about what it is possible to fit into your lunch break. If you find yourself scampering back to your desk bathed in perspiration, then some of the benefits will be lost. If you are in the habit of working in the evening, try scheduling an exercise session as the

last activity of your working day – no more work to be done after this point. It makes an excellent boundary between work and relaxation, and prevents the tendency for your work to drift later and later into the evening.

6. *Set yourself targets.* Many of the benefits of exercise are too long-term to provide day-to-day motivation. Working to a target raises the importance of your regular exercise sessions and provides a yardstick against which to measure progress. The choice of target will depend on you and your current level of fitness – it should be challenging but achievable. Beware of setting timescales that are too ambitious. Injury is a frequent consequence of exercise programmes that are increased too rapidly. A weekly increase in activity of no more than 10 per cent is often presented as a rule of thumb.

what sort of exercise?

Vary your exercise to achieve a balance of the three main ingredients of physical fitness: strength, flexibility and cardiovascular efficiency. Some forms of exercise emphasise one at the expense of others. Running, for example, develops your heart, lungs and lower body strength, but neglects the upper body and limits flexibility. Yoga is great for flexibility but limited in respect of the cardiovascular system.

All exercise burns calories, but focusing too closely on the bathroom scales can be frustrating. Much of the immediate weight loss from strenuous exercise is in the form of water and has to be replaced. To lose a pound in weight requires expenditure of 3,500 to 4,000 calories, and because of changes in the proportion of muscle to fat, some people may find that their weight increases in the early stages of an exercise programme. Don't be discouraged; it's simply that muscle weighs more than fat. You will look slimmer and feel better.

You will use almost as many calories walking a mile as

running a mile. However, more intensive exercise raises your metabolism for several hours afterwards, which means that you continue to burn calories at a higher rate.

If you need others around you to provide motivation, then join a group, class or gym or participate in some form of competitive activity. But if you are happy to work alone, you may cut out time spent making arrangements and travelling. Many solitary exercisers claim that work problems fall into place and new ideas emerge while they are working out alone.

A final word of caution. If you are overweight, have been inactive for a long time or have any history of heart trouble, talk to your doctor before commencing an exercise programme.

relaxation

'Just relax.' 'Calm down.' 'Take it easy.' When you're stressed this sort of prompting, whether from yourself or others, can have the opposite effect to the one desired. Under pressure to relax, you may feel yourself tightening up still further. Relaxation is not a routine to be wheeled out just when you are under stress, but a collection of strategies to be practised and built into your day-to-day activities. If the ability to relax is a problem for you, you might benefit from some assistance by way of one of the many books, tapes or courses that are available. You might want to consider exploring other activities too – yoga, t'ai chi, or massage, for example – to find techniques that work best for you. And don't ignore the value of hobbies and other leisure activities or the importance of taking proper breaks. In our workaholic world, too many of us are crowding out those things that allow us to recharge our batteries. Your susceptibility to stress will be lowered and the quality of your work raised if you take care to ensure that relaxation is regarded as an ongoing priority.

keeping on top of your workload

Your confidence at work may be greatly affected by the extent to which you feel you are coping with your workload. A number of surveys in the last few years have pointed to over-load being an increasing problem in workplaces throughout the Western world. People in all manner of occupations have reported increased stress and a sense of helplessness as a result.

how far are you on top of your workload?

Do you:

- work excessive hours? ☐
- have difficulty finding time for family and leisure? ☐
- find it hard to determine priorities? ☐
- fail to achieve as much as you would like in your working day? ☐
- have trouble dealing with all the paperwork that comes your way? ☐
- postpone tasks you don't like? ☐

- ▓ find yourself plagued by interruptions and distractions? ☐
- ▓ work amid constant clutter? ☐
- ▓ spend valuable time on tasks that could be delegated? ☐
- ▓ have difficulty saying no to requests? ☐

Any of these common problems may have an impact in terms of reduced self-belief. Let's look at how they might be overcome.

balancing your life

Graham Jones routinely works about 60 hours a week. He is normally in the office by 8 in the morning and leaves at 6. Lunch is a sandwich snatched at his desk. He takes work home with him every evening but, despite his best intentions, always postpones tackling it until far too late. Sometimes it is after 10 when, worn out and ratty, he finally digs out his briefcase and turns to the tasks that have been niggling him all evening. He is rarely satisfied with the quality of work done at this time of day and frequently goes to bed tense and over-tired, with consequent difficulty in sleeping. At weekends he also worries about the incomplete tasks lurking in his briefcase, but tends to put off dealing with them as long as possible. Sunday evening is always spent working, and that gets the new week off to an uncomfortable start.

I scarcely need to point out Graham's problem – work has invaded the whole of his life. There is hardly any time when he is mentally free of it. If he is not actually working, then he is worrying about it, and the time spent worrying can be as stressful as the work itself. What's more, Graham's work habits – limited breaks, late-night sessions – raise serious questions about the quality of his efforts. He needs to set some boundaries on his work time, possibly spending a little longer in the office so that he doesn't have to bring work home or, if this is unavoidable, at least getting it out of the way early in the evening and the weekend. He may also need to think about developing some new leisure interests and readdressing the amount of time he spends with his family. There is a strong chance that Graham could work fewer hours and be more productive if he took a proper lunch break and refrained from low-quality sessions such as his late-evening guilt trips.

Ask yourself:

▓ Are there any issues of work/home/leisure balance in my life?
▓ If so, what might I do to address them?

---

deciding what's important

When you are bombarded every day with an assortment of tasks, other people's requirements, distractions and interruptions, discriminating between the important and the trivial can be difficult. But clarity about priorities is important if you are to get on top of the job. Indeed, it is often suggested that 80 per cent of results come from 20 per cent of the effort. You need to be sure that you are focusing your attention and energy on the key 20 per cent.

Look at Figure 11.1. Every demand upon your time can be placed in one of the sectors according to its importance and urgency.

▓ **Sector A: tasks that are important and urgent**
Items that are both important and urgent are the ones to give immediate attention to. They are the tackle-

first items in your schedule. But it's always worth asking yourself whether better planning might have reduced their urgency.

▮ **Sector B: tasks that are important but not urgent**
These are things that must not be ignored. They are often concerned with longer-term objectives and you should ensure that you find the time to progress them. Given inadequate attention, category B tasks may suddenly be promoted to extreme category A when a deadline looms. Plan your time effectively to reduce this possibility.

▮ **Sector C: tasks that are urgent but unimportant**
Don't let these draw your attention away from those in group B. Just because they are urgent doesn't make them any more important. They may be tasks to delegate or quietly forget about.

▮ **Sector D: tasks that are neither important nor urgent**
You shouldn't be wasting time and energy on these. Frequently, tasks in this category are used as self-generated distractions – excuses for not getting down to other more important work that is viewed with some degree of apprehension. Recognise them for what they are and focus your efforts on tasks in the other sectors.

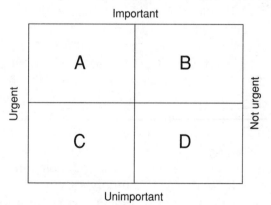

Figure 11.1 *Setting priorities*

Define your overall objectives clearly and keep them in view throughout your working week. Make sure that you achieve a balance between the different elements of your job, and don't get side-tracked into one activity to the detriment of others.

planning your schedule

Being clear about your priorities is the start of getting on top of your workload, but you also need to plan and track your time effectively. Time planning is sometimes made into a bigger deal than it needs to be. There are three essential elements to doing it well:

1. *Maintain a view over different time frames.* Try to plan with decreasing levels of specificity over the next day, the next week and the next couple of months. This way you keep a grip on your immediate commitments without losing sight of the longer-term issues that generally need to be progressed alongside the day-to-day stuff.

2. *Realistically assess the amount of time each task will take.* If you want the confidence that comes from achieving what you set out to do each day, then it's important to have a handle on how long things are going to take. Over-optimism about what can be achieved within a certain time frame is a problem. So work on it. Make a practice of estimating the expected time commitment alongside items on your 'things to do' list, and learn by experience when tasks take a greater or lesser time than expected. Give attention also to fitting the task to the available time. There are some tasks that you can only set about if you have a significant amount of time available. You need to get

yourself mentally attuned, gather resources together and make sure you are free of interruptions. There is no point in trying to gear up for such a task when you only have a short period available. So free the time you need for the longer tasks and slot the short tasks into those spare moments between other commitments.

3. *Undertake tasks at appropriate times of day.* It is difficult for any of us to maintain a constant level of attention throughout our working day. We all have body rhythms characterised by peaks and troughs of energy and alertness. You will achieve more, and reap the confidence benefits of achievement, if you schedule your most demanding tasks at times when you are best able to cope with them. If you haven't thought about energy peaks before, take a few days to observe yourself. Try to note the times when you are at your best. We are all different. For some, first thing in the morning will be a peak, but others take a while to warm up.

Most tasks will fall into one of three broad groups:

- ▒ *maintenance tasks* – those routine jobs that are essential to keep you functioning properly – staying informed, dealing with the normal inflow and outflow of information, organising your workspace, filing, completing routine returns;
- ▒ *people tasks* – negotiating, participating in meetings, persuading, reviewing performance, networking, disciplining, presenting, training, inducting, interviewing;
- ▒ *creative, planning and problem-solving tasks* – preparing plans and project briefs, writing reports, analysing results and drawing conclusions, finding solutions to problems.

I have simply given a few examples for each group. Depending on the nature of your job, there will be others appropriate to you.

Generally speaking, the maintenance tasks will make the most limited energy demands. Planning and problem-solving skills will normally require the greatest amount of concentrated attention and also larger blocks of time because of the need to get yourself up to speed before you are able to make significant progress. People tasks may be of long or short duration, but are frequently the ones that make the greatest demands on emotional energy. Those that may involve an element of confrontation are particularly tricky. If you have several of these tasks, try tackling them together – one after the other. The head of steam you build up to tackle the first helps to carry you through the subsequent ones and, overall, you will find it less emotionally draining than having to gear yourself up for each one individually.

more time-planning tips

▨ Take five minutes to review tomorrow's schedule at the end of each day. That way you start the next morning clear about what you aim to achieve and are able to hit the ground running.

▨ Use the same approach for weekly planning. A short session every Friday afternoon is a good way to map out the upcoming week. What will you need to prepare on Tuesday for that meeting on Wednesday? How much time can you spare each day to carry forward a major assignment?

▨ Crossing completed items off a list of things to do is very satisfying and helps to keep you on track, but resist the temptation to fill your list with lots of little tasks that are simply there to be crossed off.

▥ Remember that we all have a tendency to overestimate
the time needed to complete tasks we dislike, and to
underestimate the ones we like.
▥ You will never achieve time-planning perfection, so stay
flexible and deal with whatever the day throws at you.

tracking your time

Tracking is about keeping on top of the activities you have
planned – ensuring that you are reminded when actions are due
and monitoring progress towards achievement of your objectives. An electronic or PC-based organiser can greatly assist,
but whatever method of tracking you use, it needs to be simple
and workable for you. Avoid keeping information in multiple
locations – separate diaries, for example. If it is essential to
have information in different formats, make sure that there is
one master record.

postponing action

There will always be tasks that you have to put off, but
habitual procrastination is a practice arising primarily from
fear and anxiety:

▥ fear of failing or making a mistake;
▥ fear of confronting a problem;
▥ concern that you don't have the necessary information
to complete the task;
▥ uncertainty over how to go about it;
▥ anxiety about the possible consequences of an action;
▥ perfectionism – unwillingness to start a task unless it
can be completed perfectly.

If you suffer from a tendency to procrastinate, then without
some effort to break the habit you will find your effectiveness
impaired and your confidence diminished.

how to beat it

■ Own up to it and identify the real reason why you are postponing the task.

■ Schedule times for tackling difficult and unpleasant tasks.

■ Tackle boredom by allowing yourself short controlled breaks, but don't give up on the task itself.

■ Note the frequency with which tasks you have been avoiding turn out less fearsome than expected. Use this knowledge as a reference to help overcome future anxieties.

■ Recognise when you have the means to achieve a good job. Don't strive after perfection.

■ Reward yourself for successfully dealing with difficult tasks.

■ Look for the easiest point of entry to those tasks where you are unsure how to get started. You don't always have to start at the beginning.

■ Set your own deadlines for tasks that are not externally imposed.

handling information

Many of the problems of the information overload that so bedevils the modern workplace are down to fear. We copy material unnecessarily to one another for fear of being accused of failure to communicate. We hang on to items just in case they may be needed. Fearful of missing important nuggets and making mistakes as a result, we over-research and surround ourselves with excessive information. But more information is no guarantee of increased effectiveness. Beyond a certain point it has a declining marginal value, and information is of no value at all if there is so much of it that it cannot be interpreted and used. It's important to develop systematic and decisive information-handling habits. Use the four-question overload-beating routine on pages 130 and 131 for dealing with every document, letter, memo or e-mail you receive.

controlling intruders

It's hard to stay on top of your workload if you are constantly being interrupted. Not only is there the actual time lost through the interruption but, more importantly, the effort of getting back to the original task and refocusing attention. You will never be able to get rid of interruptions entirely, but you can do a lot to reduce them, and to make those remaining as brief and purposeful as possible.

Here are some suggestions:

- Use voice mail effectively to screen telephone calls. Alternatively, think about a reciprocal arrangement with colleagues whereby you take messages for one another on occasions when you need to work on a task uninterrupted.
- Set regular times each day when you will deal with those tasks that require uninterrupted concentration and will be unavailable for meetings, calls and other intrusions. Stick to it rigidly and others will come to recognise it.
- Be firm with self-generated interruptions. Recognise them as another form of procrastination.
- Help to foster a climate conducive to effective work by treating colleagues as you would have them treat you. Don't expect people to refrain from interrupting you, if you are in the habit of interrupting them.
- Consider working from home for a day when you have a task that requires concentrated thought.
- Group small tasks such as telephone calls together, to avoid them becoming separate interruptions to your flow.

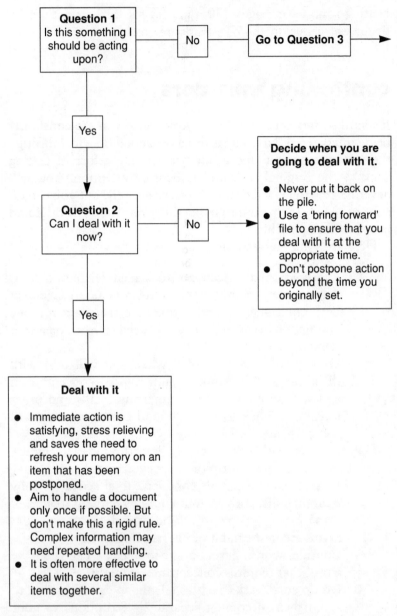

Figure 11.2 *Managing the inflow*

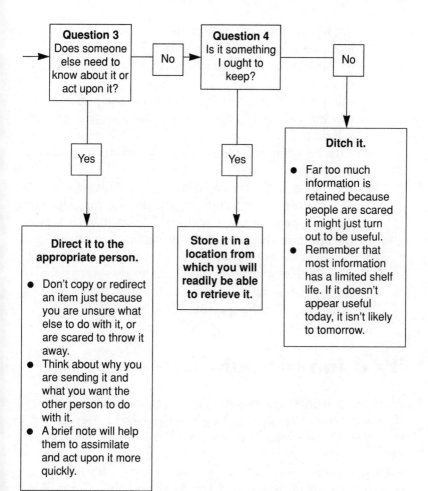

▨ Close your door, if you have one, or position your desk and office furniture to avoid giving your working area an appearance that invites passers-by to walk in and sit down.

▨ Put a time limit on interruptions. Let the person interrupting you know that you can only spare, say, five minutes.

▨ Risk being considered rude by not inviting interrupters to sit down.

▨ Encourage colleagues to come with a bullet-point note of what they want to talk to you about. This helps you to tune into the issue quickly and deters more frivolous interruptions because of the preparation involved.

▨ Give attention to your body language, and the verbal cues within a conversation that allow you to bring interruptions to a quick conclusion without unduly offending the other person.

it's a jumble out there

A cluttered workspace may indicate more than just untidiness. It may be both a result and a cause of reduced confidence. As we have already seen, anxiety about discarding material or hesitancy about what to do with it stops us acting decisively with paperwork and leads us to hang on to rubbish. But all those consequent heaps of paper, bulging files and crammed in-trays promote further uncertainty. The sheer volume and disorganisation mean that we are incapable of ordering and prioritising our workloads. Within the same pile there may be vital information and complete junk. It all shares a common fate – its importance only considered when it arrives at the top of the pile.

Other confidence-damaging effects are:

▨ distraction – with a cluttered desk there is a tendency

    to flit from task to task rather than devoting the concentrated effort needed to complete one;
■ time wasted searching for things;
■ stress – the looming presence of paper piles indicating dozens of tasks to be done is often more stressful than completing the tasks themselves.

It is possible to get into a vicious spiral of clutter resulting in progressively deeper levels of disorganisation (see Figure 11.3).
    You can free yourself from this clutter spiral by combining a campaign to introduce more decisive paper-handling habits along the lines set out earlier in this chapter with a blitz on your workspace.

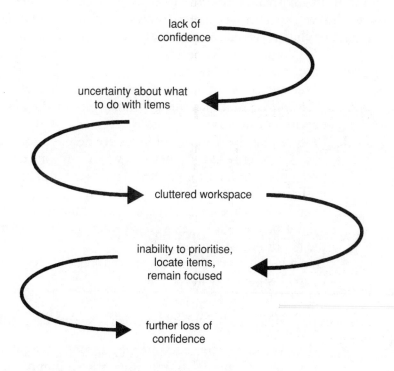

lack of
confidence

uncertainty about what
to do with items

cluttered workspace

inability to prioritise,
locate items,
remain focused

further loss of
confidence

Figure 11.3   *Spiral of clutter*

mounting a workspace blitz

Don't tackle your desktop first. Start with the cupboards and drawers furthest away from your desk – they are likely to have the largest proportion of rubbish – and move inwards towards your desk. This way you free up space for material that is currently crowding out more immediate working areas. Work through all your cupboards and drawers, discarding junk, grouping like items together and making sure that files are clearly labelled.

Simplicity has to be the keynote of your desk organisation. The accessories and equipment on your desktop should be those you use daily. Other items may be kept close to hand but away from your main working surface. Give yourself plenty of space to work. There is a psychological advantage to the absence of clutter as well as a physical one.

getting rid of the piles of paper

1. Take four empty filing trays and label them: *Action, Distribute, Read, File*. Get an empty bin for the most important category – *ditch it*!

2. Resolve that the majority of items are destined for the bin. Whatever relevance they had when they joined the pile is likely to have diminished. Don't repeat previous indecisiveness. If in doubt, throw it out.

3. Don't waste time reading items. Just skimming them should be enough to tell you whether they belong in the bin or one of the four trays.

4. Don't get distracted by acting on things as you go. Keep blasting away at the pile.

5. Zip through magazines and periodicals, and tear out the pages with articles you want to keep. Throw the rest away.

6. When you have worked your way through the piles, turn your attention to the four trays. Empty the *Distribute* tray straight away and allocate time slots to deal with the other three.

handing it over

Greater use of delegation can make a great difference to the demands upon you, but it should not be simply a knee-jerk reaction to your own overload. Try to see it not as a matter of offloading tasks you don't want to do, but as a contribution to overall productivity by placing responsibility and the necessary authority and resources where they can be discharged most effectively. You will have difficulty in delegating if you can't trust the people who work for you, or if you cannot believe that anyone else is able to do the job as well as you.

The choice of responsibilities to delegate will normally centre on those things that others may do more quickly, more cheaply or more expertly than you, or tasks that can readily be performed within the context of another person's existing job. Beware of the natural tendency to load the willing horses, or to delegate tasks only to those who have fulfilled similar work in the past.

You have to be ready to spend some time preparing colleagues for what you want them to do. This comes hard when the reason you are delegating is because of time pressure upon you. But it is a matter of short-term pain for long-term gain. If you don't set the arrangement up properly, you are likely to have disgruntled colleagues feeling they have been dumped on, or people unclear about what is expected of them. You will need to:

- set clear objectives;
- sell the benefits from the point of view of the person taking on the work;
- give the necessary authority and resources and let the other person get on with it.

This last point is the most difficult aspect of delegation. You want to get somebody to take on a responsibility, but you are reluctant to let go of the reins. You must do so. If you don't, it will remain essentially your responsibility, for which you have simply contracted out part of the donkey-work. When problems occur, they will wind up back on your plate.

turning it down

If you always say yes to requests that come your way, then you lose control of your workload. You overburden yourself and, by saying yes to unimportant requests, may find yourself unable to fulfil key features of your job. So how do you refuse? An erstwhile colleague of mine used to find it so difficult that he would invent excuses to leave meetings before the crucial moment. 'I thought you were going to ask me to do something and I was afraid that "yes" would come out,' he once admitted.

There are several reasons why saying no may be difficult. You don't want to get a reputation for negativity or perhaps to spoil your career prospects, and there is a natural tendency to avoid displeasing others or hurting their feelings. It may be that you underestimate the increased work pressure you will be under as a result of saying yes or perhaps you simply don't realise that saying no is an option.

If you are in the process of establishing a reputation, you may need to say yes more often than is good for you, but it is important to be able to draw the line skilfully and assertively, and recognise that turning down a request is not something you should apologise for or feel guilty about.

It is often difficult to weigh up these factors and give an instant response. If the required commitment is a significant one, asking for a little time to consider it is a sensible thing to do, and demonstrates that you are not dismissing the request out of hand. But don't use thinking time as an excuse to avoid making a decision at all.

Take particular care with requests where the commitment asked of you is not immediate, but comes at some time in the

If you're uncertain about a proposed new commitment, ask your-self a few questions:

- ▓ Does this form a core element of my job?
- ▓ Will my career prospects be affected if I don't do it?
- ▓ What else might I need to drop or postpone in order to undertake this? What will be the effect of that on other elements of my job?
- ▓ What might be the effect on my general lifestyle – significantly increased stress, unreasonable intrusion on my leisure time?
- ▓ Will I miss out on any opportunity to develop a new skill if I don't do this?

future – a request to make a presentation or deliver a paper at a conference, for example. When the event is three months away, it's easy to be over-optimistic about the time you will have to fit in the necessary preparation. But as the day approaches and you find your schedule ever more crowded, the additional task assumes the status of unwelcome addition to a heavy workload, and you end up resentfully turning out a rush job that doesn't do you justice. Clarity about your future commitments and a firm handle on your priorities are the way to ensure that if 'yes' does come out, it's because you want it to.

three ways to say 'no'

1. **Aggressive**
   Complain loudly about being overburdened and taken for granted. Accuse the person making the request of being unreasonable, make veiled references to other people who don't pull their weight and then burst into tears or storm out of the room.

2. **Timid**

   Mumble a response liberally laced with apologies and excuses, but stop short of using the word 'no'. Complain to colleagues later, and waste time and energy fretting about the request, but end up carrying out the task resentfully.

3. **Assertive**

   Let it be known that you are pleased to be asked, but explain succinctly and politely why you are unable to respond positively. Suggest possible alternative ways of getting the task done, and indicate any support you may be able to offer whoever takes it on.

No prizes here. Option three is the one to go for. The person making the request is under no misapprehension about your response or the reasons for it, but does not come away from the encounter angry and browbeaten; and you do not damage your positive reputation.

appearing confident

There is an infectious element to confidence. By giving attention to appearing confident, you can alter other people's reaction to you. They treat you as a confident individual and that response allows you to feel more in control, and genuinely to become more confident. In this chapter we shall consider five elements that can affect how confident you appear:

- posture;
- voice and manner of speaking;
- body language;
- image and clothing;
- being yourself.

posture

A slumped posture gives the impression of a cowed and beaten demeanour, while one that is overly rigid can indicate tension, anxiety and uncertainty. But poor posture does not just convey an air of limited confidence. It can affect our breathing and hence our speech. Muscular tension, particularly in the back and neck, resulting from incorrect posture can be a source of considerable discomfort and inability to relax.

Correct posture is balanced, relaxed and does not subject any part of the body to excess gravity. We grow used to poor posture over the years and may often be completely unaware of the way we appear to others or of the problems we may be causing ourselves. We come to regard our customary way of holding ourselves as natural and normal and any other sort of posture as strange and uncomfortable. It is not generally sufficient just to tell yourself to straighten up or loosen up. By way of a quick posture check, try the following.

Stand in a comfortable, relaxed position, hands by your sides. If you are maintaining a good balanced posture your ear lobe should be directly above the middle of your shoulder and your hip joint. Continuing that same line downwards, it would pass through a point just behind your kneecap and at the front of your ankle. Your feet should be shoulder-width apart with your weight balanced evenly between the heels and balls of your feet.

Get someone else to check you out or stand in front of a mirror. If the stance I have described is not your normal one, then it is likely to feel rather strange. Balanced posture is, of course, just as important whether we are standing, seated or moving, but it is not easy to correct ingrained bad habits on your own. You may wish to get some assistance with adjusting your posture and ensuring that it serves you well at all times. One of the best-known methods is the Alexander technique. This regime concentrates on restoring good use of our bodies by relearning ways of holding ourselves in everyday activities, and puts particular emphasis on coordination and balance of the head, neck and back. There are a number of books available, but one-to-one sessions with a skilled practitioner are generally recommended. Other activities such as Pilates and yoga can also have a very beneficial effect.

Be conscious that postural difficulties may become more acute when you are under stress. In my case, I have a tendency to tighten my shoulder muscles at such times, and it is necessary for me to give extra attention to relaxing them. Of course, pressure periods are the times when balance and relaxation are particularly important – so monitor your posture under tough conditions as well as easy ones, to be sure that it isn't letting you down when you need it most.

voice

Our voices reveal a great deal about the confidence, or lack of it, we may be experiencing. There are a number of give-away signs of tension and anxiety:

- 'strangled' speech as a result of tense neck and throat muscles;
- weak and wobbly voice emanating from the changed breathing patterns that occur when we are nervous;
- tension in the jaw and lips producing a rather terse style of delivery as well as a 'buttoned up' appearance;
- nervous gabble;
- rising pitch at the end of sentences, giving the impression of hesitancy and uncertainty.

A confident, well-projected voice is not a matter of forcing the sounds out at increased volume – that will, if anything, increase tension and distortion. It requires that you pay attention to posture, breathing and relaxation of important muscles. If you know that you will be required to speak in a situation that is likely to be stressful – difficult meeting, interview, presentation – go through the following brief routine just beforehand:

1. Check your posture. It should be balanced and relaxed, in the manner discussed in the previous section.
2. Relax your neck and shoulders – waggle your shoulders, nod your head slowly several times and then let any tension drain away.

3. Tense the muscles in your jaw for a few seconds; then let go and feel them relax.
4. Take several long, slow, deep breaths. Let each exhalation come in the form of a long, deep sigh that takes away any remaining tension with it.

The breathing is the most important part of this routine. So if you don't have time for the rest – or you're in a public place where you would feel self-conscious nodding your head and waggling your shoulders – at least do the breathing bit.

While you are speaking, try to maintain breathing that fully utilises your lungs, not just the upper chest area. When we are stressed and nervous, our breathing becomes shallow and more rapid – not conducive to strong, confident speech. Visualise your voice as being supported from the abdominal area, not just coming from the upper regions of your chest and throat.

delivery

Nervousness often results in a tendency to gabble. Our mouths seem to run at a faster pace than our brains and what comes out is not quite what we had intended. We are conscious that we're not expressing ourselves very well, straying off the point, talking too quickly, but we feel unable to stem the flow of words.

Preparation and pacing are the way to attack nervous gabble. Think beforehand about what you are going to say. Write down the main points that you want to get across in the order you want to make them. Just noting down half a dozen key words will help to keep you on track. When you speak, resist the urge to embark on subsidiary arguments and justifications that you hadn't planned. Unless you are completely in charge of your material you are liable to lose your way. Stick to the main points and express them clearly and simply. Planning like this is not just for formal presentations. You can use it when you have a difficult phone call, for example. Even when you are in meetings and required to respond to what other people are saying, it's possible to jot down a few key words representing the points you want to make. When your turn comes to speak, you are able to keep yourself focused.

Effective pacing will help you to express yourself clearly and give valuable thinking time. Nervous gabbling (as opposed to excited gabbling) is a low-confidence activity – trying to gallop through what you have to say as quickly as possible in order to get out of the limelight. So start by asserting your right to hold people's attention while you speak. Slow down your speech and pause between thoughts more often. When responding to questions, give yourself some thinking time before you pitch in – the quality of your answers will be improved. And use questions yourself. Asking a question or seeking clarification on a question you have just been asked is a good way to grab a bit of space to get your thoughts together. Don't expect to switch to better-paced speech instantly. You will need to work at it, and some practice with a tape recorder may be useful, but the benefits in terms of more effective presentation and commanding presence should be worth the effort.

body language

Body language speaks volumes about our confidence. Unfortunately, it is not easy to control without a great deal of practice, perhaps one reason why it is such a powerful communicator. It is hard when you are under pressure to give attention to what your hands, eyes and posture are telling people, but there are some things that you should particularly try to bear in mind.

eye contact

Everybody knows that eye contact is important in communication. We look to the eyes to confirm whether what is being said can be relied upon as accurate. Is the speaker telling the truth, exaggerating, afraid, sincere, angry, genuinely sorry, truly enthusiastic, ashamed? When we are unable to make eye contact with somebody who is speaking to us, concerns start to arise. It has been shown that in interviews, for example, unease starts to develop on the part of the interviewer when eye contact occurs for less than 50 per cent of the time.

Absence of eye contact is associated with having something to hide. People who fail to meet our eyes sufficiently may be regarded as shifty or untrustworthy. In fact, low levels of eye contact may result from nothing more than shyness. If you are affected, then you will need to work on making more frequent eye contact a normal feature of conversation. Some people find that it helps to practise speaking in front of a mirror. However, don't go overboard on eye contact. Too much can be as discomforting as too little, as you will know if you have ever had a conversation with one of those intense, eyeballing types who like to subject you to an unwavering gaze.

When speaking to a number of people, at a presentation for example, take care that you are not focusing on just one or two individuals. Try to sweep your audience with your gaze. If you are dealing with just a small number of people, try to make eye contact with all of them, not just those who may be smiling or signifying their approval in some way. Pay particular attention to any who may be fidgeting or looking bored.

position and movement

We have already seen the importance of posture in presentation of ourselves, but how we move and hold our limbs also has a considerable impact on the extent to which we appear confident to others. Jerky movements, nervous mannerisms, fidgeting and fiddling with objects such as pens or fashion accessories are all signs of unease. Smoothness and fluidity of movement demonstrate confidence and control. Prepare for nerve-racking events such as interviews and presentations by use of visualisation techniques. Picture yourself moving in a smooth, calm and relaxed manner. If you are inclined to gesticulate or display nervous hand movements, you might want to practise speaking while sitting on your hands. Remember to take them out when the real event comes around! Concern about nervousness causing your hands to shake may be overcome by placing them together, but don't clasp them too tightly or wring them.

The way you hold your limbs is also revealing. A compact posture – arms tucked in, feet and knees together – shows submissiveness. Adopt a more open and expansive posture to radiate confidence. Folded arms are a classic sign of protectiveness. Such a closed position indicates either that individuals don't want to be in the situation they find themselves in, or that there are aspects of themselves that they do not wish to reveal.

generating rapport through body language

There are some simple ways in which you can help to generate rapport in one-to-one situations through your awareness of body language. Leaning forward slightly when the other person is speaking indicates an interest in what he or she is saying. Mirroring the body language of the other person helps to build up rapport. You can observe mirroring just by watching people engaged in conversation. Where a clear rapport has been established you will notice both parties unconsciously producing very similar body movements. One puts hands behind the head and leans back in the chair; the other does likewise. To a certain extent you can use conscious mirroring to help build rapport, but don't go too far. These are subtle and normally unconscious responses. Try too hard and you run the risk that the other person will notice and assume mimicry.

clothing and image

Once upon a time the choice of work clothes was an easy matter. It was a case of appearing in the appropriate uniform – dark business suit, male or female variety, and sensible accessories. Ironically, the modern trend towards dressing down in the office, aimed at allowing people to feel more comfortable and creative, has resulted in greater levels of uncertainty and potential for loss of confidence. Faced with relaxation of the old rules, people are not quite sure where they stand. Many companies that have introduced dressing-down policies have found it necessary to issue guidelines on which forms of casual dress are acceptable and which not.

So what is the key to feeling confident about your appearance at work? I hate to say it but generally it is about ensuring that you are not striking a discordant note. For all that we want to be seen as individuals, we seldom want to look out of place in a work setting. Having said that, giving your work appearance a makeover can increase your confidence tremendously, especially when a change of work clothing and hairstyle coincides with other confidence-boosting efforts. It presents an external commitment to change that gives leverage to any modifications you are making to habits, routines or attitudes.

I have neither the space nor the expertise to embark on a detailed study of image generation through clothes, cosmetics and hairstyle, but there are plenty of books and professional consultants prepared to offer advice. When thinking about confident dressing, take account of what sort of impression you want to create and whether it is appropriate to the environment in which you are working. Give thought to fabrics, cut, patterns and colours that will make the best of your size, shape and colouring. To maintain your confidence on those occasions when you are not sure what to expect in terms of dress standards, ensure that you have at least one 'go anywhere' outfit – something in which you will not look out of place regardless of what other people are wearing.

being yourself

The final recommendation in this chapter has to be about behaving naturally. We all play slightly different roles in the various situations we encounter, but is your 'at work' persona one that you are happy with? It's possible to become too preoccupied with what you think other people expect of you and to lose touch with the sense of being yourself. But if you are trying to present yourself in a manner that doesn't feel comfortable or natural to you, then you will not be convincing. It's back to our familiar theme of being in control. When you are comfortable with yourself, you are in control. When you are working to perceptions of what you think other people expect, they are in control.

conclusion

So there you have it. A brief excursion through the most common threats to our workplace confidence. I hope that reading the book has provided you with some useful tools for maintaining your resilience, overcoming challenges and bouncing back from disappointments. But don't expect instant fixes. Be prepared to persist with the strategies that appeal to you and recognise that maintaining your confidence will never be a one-off activity. Around every corner there lurks a fresh challenge. You may never achieve total confidence in everything you do, but perhaps that is not a bad thing. The day you cease to have any apprehension about new challenges is probably the day you have become too complacent.

When you are feeling under threat, it's easy to run away with the idea that you are the only one who ever suffered a decline in self-belief. But talk to people about confidence. You will find that nobody is as confident as they would like to be. Own up to feelings of nervousness and apprehension and even those who appear the most outwardly assured will admit to the same susceptibilities. The simple recognition that we are all in the same boat when it comes to confidence can strengthen your resolve enormously.

And one final word: don't forget that confidence is a commodity that grows in the using. If you wait for the confidence to come to you before you are prepared to embark on a course of action, then you will wait a long time. Take your courage in both hands and go for it!

Good luck.

other titles in the Kogan Page creating success series

Be Positive by Phil Clements
Business Etiquette by David Robinson
Develop Your Assertiveness by Sue Bishop
Develop Your NLP Skills by Andrew Bradbury
Developing Your Staff by Patrick Forsyth
E-Business Essentials by Matt Haig
Empowering People by Jane Smith
How to Beat Your Competitors by John G Fisher
How to Generate Great Ideas by Barrie Hawkins
How to Manage Organisational Change by D E Hussey
How to Motivate People by Patrick Forsyth
How to Run a Successful Conference by John G Fisher
How to Write a Marketing Plan by John Westwood
Improve Your Communication Skills by Alan Barker
Improving Employee Performance by Nigel Harrison
Make Every Minute Count by Marion E Hayes
Make That Call! by Iain Maitland
Making Innovation Happen by Michael Morgan
Organise Yourself by John Caunt
Performance Appraisals by Bob Havard
Successful Presentation Skills by Andrew Bradbury
Successful Project Management by Trevor Young
Team Building by Robert B Maddux
Using the Internet Faster and Smarter by Brooke Broadbent
Write That Letter! by Iain Maitland
Writing Effective E-mail by Nancy Flynn and Tom Flynn

forthcoming titles

Communication at Work by Judith Taylor
How to Write a Business Plan by Brian Finch
Taking Minutes of Meetings by Joanna Gutmann

Visit Kogan Page on-line

Comprehensive information on
Kogan Page titles

Features include

■ complete catalogue listings,
  including book reviews and
  descriptions

■ on-line discounts on a variety
  of titles

■ special monthly promotions

■ information and discounts on
  NEW titles and BESTSELLING titles

■ a secure shopping basket facility
  for on-line ordering

■ infoZones, with links and
  information on specific areas of
  interest

PLUS everything you need to know
about KOGAN PAGE

http://www.kogan-page.co.uk